T0368425

God Saved
the Best for Last,
or Waterbugs Turn Into
Blessings

SUSIE LIND

WestBow Press books may be ordered through booksellers or by contacting:

WestBow Press
A Division of Thomas Nelson & Zondervan
1663 Liberty Drive
Bloomington, IN 47403
www.westbowpress.com
844-714-3454

All Scripture quotations are taken from the Holy Bible, NEW INTERNATIONAL VERSION®, NIV®
Copyright © 1973, 1978, 1984, 2011 by Biblica, Inc.® Used by permission. All rights reserved worldwide.

ISBN: 979-8-3850-2887-0 (sc)
ISBN: 979-8-3850-2888-7 (e)

Library of Congress Control Number: 2024913510

Print information available on the last page.

WestBow Press rev. date: 8/22/2024

PROLOGUE

To my family and friends, this is my story as I remember it from when I left home in 1962 until I married Dwight 15 years ago. I've skimmed over things that are not pertinent, but hope I have hit the highlights of the most significant experiences. Laugh and rejoice with me that God turns water bugs—those unpleasant cockroaches that live in water and moisture—into blessings. Just as they make use of a place to stay afloat, surface tension kept me afloat, but barely.

God Saved the Best for Last grew out of a desire to communicate the unusual path God led me on as a young woman during an 11-year quest for independence that ended in total dependence on God.

I was determined to manage my own life. God granted me a measure of success as a secretary in the U.S. Department of State Foreign Service, assigned to embassies in a number of countries. He returned goodness for my rebellion and defiance, and He brought me back to His feet gradually.

My quest for independence led to total dependence upon God. I resigned from the U.S. Department of State Foreign Service and became a missionary with HCJB Global (now Reach Beyond) on June 8, 1973. Though not all my questions were answered, and not all of my choices were the best, God has been my closest friend. He's the one I depend on for guidance and sustenance. My journey has been one of learning daily obedience and faith. I would not know how to live any other way.

My hope is that you will thank God with me for avoiding a very different life than I might have had without God.

Susie Lind

CONTENTS

CHAPTER 1

Water Bugs and a Shared Bath

The early-morning ride was quiet. Dad drove me to the Greyhound bus station in downtown Cleveland. He had been angry about my decision to leave home, though I was in my early 20s. One of his arguments was, "You can't afford to live on what InterVarsity can pay you." To that I said, "I'll find out what everyone else does and do the same thing." Dad did not like to lose an argument, so he said that if I left home, I didn't need to come back. My father could be my best friend or my greatest adversary—he kept me guessing which it would be until the day I left home in September 1962.

As my two suitcases were put on the bus, Dad's last words were, "Well, kid, if you don't like it, or if it doesn't work out, you can always come back home in a year." Then he asked how much money I had. I forget how much it was, but he knew it was not very much, so he handed me five $20 bills. I hugged him and got on the bus to Chicago, eager to join the InterVarsity headquarters staff.

In my growing-up years, lots of missionaries stayed in our home when they came to speak in my home church. One of the more vivid memories I have is of Geoffrey Bull, a former missionary to Tibet, who was imprisoned for several years because of his faith. He stayed in our home twice, telling us a bit more about his experiences each time. My parents entertained constantly, and I enjoyed looking at all the signatures in their guest books. I think I learned something from every missionary or preacher who stayed with us.

In my sophomore year at Case Western Reserve University, I had been part of an on-campus InterVarsity chapter of Christian students meeting weekly to discuss how to live the Christian life and how to help others find Jesus as their Savior. At that time, I did not know what I wanted to do with my life, but when I heard about an upcoming Urbana convention, I wanted to go. I even took a difficult babysitting job for a week in order to earn what I needed for the three days.

I found a student who planned to drive to Urbana-Champaign for the weekend, who was looking for more riders to help pay for his gas. Students who wanted to take some time during their Christmas break went to the event for a spiritual challenge. We drove from Cleveland to southern Illinois where the University of Illinois in Urbana-Champaign turned most of the dorms and housing to IV every four years. Several of the IV staff came prepared with extra winter clothing for students who came from places such as Africa and India—not prepared for the cold climate that dumped lots of snow on the campus in December.

There were thousands of students from all over the U.S. and around the world. Most were interested in missions and had a desire for a deeper relationship with God. Counselors were on-site along with missionaries setting up displays for this unique experience where we heard the hearts of many well-known Christians. Names I had heard over the years were among those present.

The following summer I had been invited to Cedar Bay Camp Upper Peninsula run by InterVarsity for years. It was a large facility with a cold lake, and we had a wonderful time with young people my age from all over the U.S. At one point they needed someone to play the piano for a happy birthday for one of the staff—I happily agreed. For the rest of the days at Cedar Lake, I was the extra pianist. I had taken lessons from third grade right through my sophomore year in high school, taking a break for a year. Mrs. Gillette contacted my mother to let her know she would be glad to teach me another year, if I was interested. I was.

By my junior year at Case Western, I had clerked in one of our family's bakery stores long enough to be able to spend the first semester in a dorm. During that time I became even more involved with InterVarsity. My money was running out, and my grades were not great in everything, so I was faced with a decision to quit school and work. I returned home and was hired by Ohio Bell Phone Company. I liked business, but I needed more training. So I enrolled in a two-year private secretarial course at Dyke College in downtown Cleveland. Over 1,400 students were enrolled in 1995. Dyke changed its name after I left, to David N. Myers University in honor of a graduate (David N. Myer) who donated $2 million. Dyke was the first education I really enjoyed. I looked forward to every day and worked hard. Working at the bakery weekends and holidays gave me enough money to stay in school, and my parents helped pay for the last year at Dyke. My dad wanted me to work at the bakery, but that was not my call, and there were too many relatives keeping a critical eye on me as well as my cousins and my brothers.

I was just about to finish the course when Charles Hummel offered me a job as chapter secretary with InterVarsity in Chicago. Inquiring about the courses I would not finish, I realized they were to build up shorthand speed and a few other things I thought I could manage without. So I accepted the job and moved to Chicago. At the time, I thought it was great! Independence at any price was what I wanted and what I got.

Charles had visited my church in Cleveland, and because I had been very active with InterVarsity as a college student, he suggested that I consider coming to headquarters to work to use my skills. After two years of college and a year and a half of private secretarial training, I finally had a chance to use my education.

I had grown up in a Christian family and was taught that God was in control of my life, even when I didn't feel it. On the eight-hour bus ride, I asked the Lord to give me courage for the adventure I was beginning. I had no idea how much courage I would need in the coming days.

Finally, at the Chicago bus terminal, I took a cab to an address Mom had written on a piece of paper. A rooming house for Christian women was advertised in *Moody* magazine, and my parents made arrangements for me to live there. I was unfamiliar with living in a big city, and kept wondering when the office buildings would end, and I'd see some houses with grass around them. When the cab stopped at 5940 N. Kenmore, I was sure it was a mistake. Surprised by the appearance of the brownstone that was my destination, I took a deep breath, paid the cab driver, grabbed my two suitcases, and went inside.

Drawing by Susie Lind

Bessie, an elderly lady who walked with a cane, showed me to my room on the main floor. It was large, with high ceilings, a compact Pullman kitchen, a single bed, and a maroon overstuffed chair. Probably a parlor at one time, one wall had windows along it, and that night as the streetlight went on, I discovered the drapes did not meet. A heavy purple curtain covered the clothes closet. It reminded me of the veil in the temple. There was nothing cozy about the room, but I didn't notice that for a few days.

It didn't take me long to unpack. Bessie invited me to go to a delicatessen around the corner to buy some food. I didn't recall ever being in a neighborhood delicatessen before, but I had seen them in movies. As Bessie hobbled along, I followed her. She did not hear well, so conversation with her was a bit awkward. I remember looking at her and wondering if I would be just like her someday—all alone in a rooming house with a hot plate to cook on, sharing a bath.

Quickly, I discovered how limited my knowledge of homemaking was. I had no idea how to plan a menu, defrost a refrigerator, scrub a floor or successfully complete a whole load of laundry or cook a meal. Mom, a perfectionist, tried to be patient with my desire to learn how to do things, but in the end it was easier for her to do them herself. A cleaning lady kept our five-bedroom, five-bath house in good order, and the spring cleaning was done professionally.

Even pleading for a chance to use my artistic flair to paint cement blocks in the basement after a couple of floods, Mom's reply was, "What would Grandpa have to do when he comes for a visit?" She kept jobs like that for when he and Grandma came to spend a couple of weeks with us. Once, Mom let me wash the floor in the bathroom over the garage—one place company never saw.

So, here I was, alone and unprepared to manage. I fixed myself something to eat, sat down to eat it and ended up just looking at it, unable to eat. That was the first time I remember being horribly homesick. Everything in my life was unfamiliar, from my job to my living situation. But I knew *I had to stick it out.*

Getting a whole meal ready at the same time was beyond me. Often, I'd have such a wait between when the vegetables and main course were ready, that I would eat right out of the pans whenever something was cooked. This was something I never would have done at home, but I rationalized that it was just for me.

Then I remembered the list of names my parents had given me to contact. I called everyone on the list within the first few weeks I was in Chicago. The coins hardly jangled into the hallway pay phone, when a nearby door opened just enough for me to see a pair of peering eyes. That's all I knew about the lady in the room next to mine.

When I did my laundry in the basement, to save on quarters, I washed things together that I shouldn't have. Sometimes I forgot to take clothes off the basement line. Late one night I went down to get my clothes. When I turned the light on, a scurry of dark shadows moved up from the floor to the ceiling. That was my first encounter with water bugs. The walls were crawling with them! I was horrified! They were thriving on the moisture in the basement. They are easy to kill, if you can catch them. Almost every place I lived for the next 11 years had water bugs or cockroaches. They were like the sin of resentment and anger that I carried with me for years.

The biggest adjustment to life at 5940 N. Kenmore was that I shared a bath with two other ladies on the first floor, and the only one I knew was Bessie. The one who peered out of her door in the room next to mine, I never met. Before I used the tub, I scrubbed it with cleanser twice—just for good measure. The bathroom was opposite the front door of the house. Many times as I left the bathroom, I was surprised by a blast of Chicago's cold, winter air as someone left or entered the house. At home we had three bathrooms upstairs for our five bedrooms and, if for some reason they were occupied, there was the powder room off the front hallway or the bathroom in the basement. One of them was always free. I figured that I was making up for that convenience now.

After several months, a room became available on the second floor, and girls on that floor encouraged me to take it. I moved to a room next to Eva, who would become a lifelong friend. There were three of us about the same age on the second floor, and we ate together sometimes. The second floor was much sunnier than the first floor, and the ceilings were not so high, making the rooms cozier. Windows provided cross-ventilation for relief during sultry Chicago summers. Eva let me borrow her sewing machine to learn how to repair and make clothing for work. I will be forever grateful to her for her kindness. Many years later I learned to make my wardrobe: blouses, skirts, suits and underwear. As I look back at photos, I made some very expensive looking suits and dresses.

Headquarters was on the fashionable north side of downtown Chicago on North Astor Street in a large, stone house with several big rooms that had elaborate crown molding and wood paneling. The kitchen was in the basement, and the house had the first dumbwaiter I had ever seen. A former billiard room with a large fireplace was used for the chapel, and a fire in the fireplace was welcome on cold days. Shipping, the mailroom, receipting, Nurses Christian Fellowship staff and office management were on the first floor.

The second floor housed accounting offices, for Charles Hummel (who was in charge of all field staff workers), and the general director, Charles Troutman. I shared an office with the secretary to the board and Charles Hummel's secretary. On the third floor were Eric Fife and his secretary, Paul Little, and *His* magazine staff. A few years before I arrived, Joe Bayly had worked there as publisher of the magazine. These people were giants of the faith to me.

The headquarters staff was like a family. I remember staff devotions as good times that I looked forward to each week. When the ministry was in need financially, or if someone was seriously ill, we stopped our work and went to the chapel to pray. And God answered.

As chapter secretary, I handled all correspondence and some minor billing and collecting for 350 InterVarsity chapters in universities and colleges across the U.S. I learned the names and locations of most of the state colleges around the country. My secretarial skills were still pretty rough, but I had a heart to do God's work and a desire to grow spiritually. After Charles Hummel's secretary resigned, I did some secretarial work for him and enjoyed it.

Once during a board meeting at headquarters, we ran out of coffee. The secretary to the board had just gone to buy more. When one of the board members asked me for more coffee, I didn't have a clue what to do. I told him I'd make some more. I had never made coffee in my life, and he seemed pretty desperate, so I made another pot using the same grounds again. When I served the coffee, he wondered what happened to the second cup of coffee, because the first cup had tasted so good. Well, I didn't tell *him* what I had done, but I did tell the secretary when she returned.

Reflecting on this time, I suppose I thought I would work there the rest of my life and continue on that spiritual path. But something would happen that would shake my foundation and make me angry with God, sending me in another direction for several years.

CHAPTER 2

Understanding Dad

My father worked six days every week, mostly because he and his three brothers were working for their father who owned a very large bakery in northern Ohio, and an added catering business that was successful. They all worked long hours. My dad's area was maintenance of new ovens and old, assembly lines, and getting stores ready to open and keep that way. He also had first-aid training for cuts, burns, falls, etc., that occur in large businesses with several hundred employees.

I remember seeing him helping his employees learn to solder, repair plumbing, teaching the importance of avoiding certain electrical problems, so he could send them to one of our stores rather than running around himself.

But I also remember him yelling at a man who had driven too close to something and put a big dent all along a new truck. He did not use any swear words, but that might have been less painful. The rebuke had no end, so I slipped out of the office.

My earliest childhood memories were of grade school, when my grades were not good. I would sit at the top of the stairs waiting for Dad to yell at me and probably hit me. School became something I feared. By fourth grade, my mom made it a point to talk to my teacher. She made a special effort help me, but Dad kept saying, "I expect perfect grades from you!"

Grandma Pile was the key to understanding my father. When I was young my brother Larry and I stayed at the big family house with Grandma. She had the first set of colored dominoes I ever saw, and I loved playing dominoes with her. While we played at the table in the breakfast room, she gave me the insight I had needed to understand Dad.

She said that one night Grandpa Pile was angry with my father, so angry that when he started hitting my father, she took the other children into her bedroom and locked the door. She did not dare interfere or intervene. She said that was a terrible night—one she would never forget. Then I realized that my father was disciplining us (and probably the employees) the same way he had been disciplined. I didn't like the discipline any better, but at least I understood where it might have come from. Looking back, I don't remember feeling that Dad was ever pleased with me until I was nearly 30.

One evening when I was 19, going to Case Western Reserve University and living at home, I had been on campus and heard Henry Cabot Lodge addressing students for Nixon's presidential campaign. Some of what he said impressed me. That night, I brought it up (a big mistake), and Dad ended supper by hitting me on the face with his big hand. I did not dare say another word, but I looked at everyone at the table, one by one, and there was no offer for help or consolation. My cheek stung, and my emotions were numb. I quietly got up and pulled out the chair, put it back in place, and slowly walked upstairs to my room. I lay on the bed and just stayed numb for quite a long time.

I think that was when I knew I needed to move out of the house. Years later, one of my brothers brought up the situation and told me I had been very brave to just walk away. I told him that was all I could do.

For as long as I can remember, Dad attended yearly conventions in Chicago. He was a member of the American Society of Bakery Engineers (now the American Society of Baking). Their meetings were held in March when Chicago could be coldest and windiest. Mom often went with him.

Mom was curious about my living conditions, so one night Mom and Dad brought me home in a taxi. Dad waited in the taxi while Mom came inside to see where I lived. Later, Mom's best friend told me that my mother cried all the way home after seeing my room. I wouldn't have understood that at the time, because I would have thought she would be pleased to see me living on my own.

My brother Larry was a student at Wheaton College in the suburbs of Chicago and took the train from Wheaton to join Mom, Dad and me for dinner at a restaurant near the Edgewater Beach Hotel. We all had a good laugh as we watched a hot pepper fall off a waiter's tray, then get kicked around the floor from table to table. It was still being kicked around the floor when we left. Those humorous memories remind me it was not all bad.

A couple of years later, Dad was elected vice president of the American Society of Bakery Engineers, and Mom came to Chicago to give him support. There was a reception line—my first—and I stood in it with Mom and Dad. Mom was not comfortable with this kind of protocol, but Dad said to me, "There's nothing to it, kid. Just shake hands, look everyone in the eye and say something nice." I've always been grateful that he taught me how to make strangers feel at home.

It would be five years before Dad came inside of any place where I lived. Several years later, Dad not only encouraged me in my life choices, he became my biggest supporter. God gave us 12 good years before he died.

CHAPTER 3

Surviving

Stacey Woods, founder of InterVarsity was ready to retire, so the board of trustees chose Mr. Charles Troutman as the new director. He had considerable experience in Australia where he had been active with the International Fellowship of Evangelical Students (IFES).

A secretary was needed for Mr. Troutman, and I was asked if I would take the job and learn as I went. I agreed. Since I had only been there about a year, I worked thoroughly and carefully to build up friendships with the staff in Chicago and elsewhere as they contacted us. Tension began to mount as quick, private discussions began in the halls, chapel and kitchen. I felt totally at a loss to understand what was wrong.

Apparently the board of trustees did not agree that Mr. Troutman was the right choice for the job. This caused a lot of tension, and I began to think that I was on the wrong side, too.

Many of the staff at InterVarsity graciously invited me for meals in their homes. I wanted to thank several of them, so I invited a group of 7 to my newly decorated second-floor room for a spaghetti supper. This was something I thought I could afford to serve and manage by myself.

I borrowed a folding table and chairs from the office, and a friend who had a car brought guests who had no car. As people came into the room, it filled up quickly. Some had to step into the hallway to make room to set up the table and chairs in the middle of my room.

It never occurred to me that my roaster pan might not be adequate to boil enough spaghetti for eight people. Back then I didn't know about putting oil in the water to keep spaghetti from sticking together. As I cleared the plates, I nearly died of embarrassment when I saw lumpy clumps of spaghetti stuck together! They all were gracious, and no one complained.

While the table was being folded up after supper, some guests had to step back into the hallway or stand against the walls, then everyone found a place to sit wherever possible to see slides someone had brought. It was a wonderful lesson on how little was required to return hospitality to others. Afterward, Eva and I laughed about the unusual experience I had given my guests!

One of the perks of working with Mr. T was a trip to the Cedar Bay Camp with a group of staff. I looked forward to that with joy. Four of us pitched in for gasoline, because it was a long drive from Chicago to Michigan's Upper Peninsula. It was a refreshing feeling to return to the beautiful facility in the woods I had enjoyed years before as a college student for an InterVarsity camp.

I put the camp's electric typewriter on a small desk and put a pillow on the chair so I could reach the keys. If I needed to get something from my room, rather than disturb the session, I climbed out the window onto a rock below and carefully dropped onto a path.

Two of us took turns playing the piano for the staff, and what wonderful singing there was from our group of servants. What a wonderful two weeks of fellowship, and seeing God work among us.

One winter I got a high fever and was too weak to find a doctor. One of the girls from the third floor of the rooming house thought that if she gave me an alcohol bath it would help bring my fever down. Neither of us had any alcohol, but she had a bottle of Evening in Paris cologne, thinking it would serve the same purpose. The smell was so strong that I felt really sick to my stomach and ended up taking a bath, weak as I was, to get

rid of the scent. To this day, I can't stand the smell of Evening in Paris. Another of the girls asked her doctor to come to the rooming house to examine me. He prescribed something I could barely afford, but an unexpected check came from home in time to pay for the prescription and the doctor's fee.

On a Wednesday night I was waiting on the "L" platform for a train to take me to church. A group of young boys, probably 11 to 14 years of age, started smart-mouthing me, swearing, then began poking and jabbing me. I became frightened when they pushed me closer and closer to the edge of the platform as a train approached. Just before they shoved me too far, a man stepped forward from nowhere. The boys stopped. When I boarded the train, I looked for the man to thank him. He was nowhere to be seen in my car or the one in front or in back. To this day, I wonder if the man might have been an angel.

Many, many times I had enough change in my wallet to get to church, but not enough to come home. The Lord was *always* faithful. I think I only had to ask someone for a ride once in three years. I went to the church on the "L" often with another girl from the rooming house. A friend would usually meet us in her car and take us the rest of the way to church. Two ladies took turns picking us up.

The boarding house had a new resident—someone who moved into the corner room on the first floor until the Veteran Affairs hospital could admit her. No one had seen her since she moved in, but we could hear sounds as we walked past her room. A few days after she had moved in, I arrived late in the evening and found some of the girls talking quietly on the second-floor landing. Our new building manager and his wife (students at Moody Bible Institute) said that a doctor had been called to treat her, then she had been taken to the VA hospital during the night. The rumor was that she had overdosed on pills, and none of us wanted to be around if she died. We were afraid to have her in the house.

The next morning it was an icy winter day, and I bundled up for my 45-minute trip to work. There, in the hallway, outside her room, stood this lady of mystery, in her pajamas, rope in hand. I was sure she was going to hang herself. I was afraid to return after work, so delayed getting home.

After slowing down my return home from work with various stops, I approached the house from the back alley. If there were police cars in front of the house, I would not go home but go elsewhere for a while. Slowly, I approached the house. To my amazement, I saw the rope strung across the back yard and the pajamas hanging on it. Now, how she managed to wear them and hang them at the same time is still a mystery!

Another interesting renter on the third floor caused a stir. A woman under psychiatric care had moved to a third-floor room. She called her psychiatrist on the pay phone in the third-floor hallway—not a very private place—and what the girls overheard as she described her dreams of murdering someone would have raised anyone's eyebrows. No one stayed around to hear details. At night she frightened the third-floor ladies darting around in the hallway like a caged bird, stopping at each bedroom door, standing quietly, casting a shadow under each person's door.

Around this time a young couple moved into the basement apartment and became caretakers of the rooming house. The girls on the third floor asked for locks on their bedroom doors. Until the locks were installed, they used chairs to secure the doors at night. The girl eventually left.

During the three years I lived in the rooming house, I accepted all invitations to go anywhere. I visited my brother Larry in Wheaton as often as I could, and I enjoyed visiting my cousin, Ann Beattie, who was teaching in the suburbs. The change was refreshing. Larry found it a novelty to visit me at the rooming house and came with a classmate once. In retrospect, most of my friends thought the rooming house was worse than unique—what I thought it was—and wondered why I continued to live there so long. Good question!

One of the funniest incidents during my InterVarsity years happened while the board members were eating supper in the chapel. I was helping to serve the supper. One of the shortest men on staff was sitting at the end of a folding table. At some point in the meal, the table legs at his end started to collapse. To keep the board members from noticing it, he supported the table with his knees by pressing his toes against the floor the rest of the meal, all while trying to cut meat and act as though nothing was wrong.

The Troutmans became my mentors. He was one of the kindest men I ever knew. He and his wife had a wonderful worldview of missions, and I caught it. It was great to observe the family interacting with one another, openly and honestly as well as with kindness. I saw how deep their faith was, trusting God in everything. Mr. T, who had grown up in Arizona, often talked about the West. The more I heard about the

West, the more I wanted to see it for myself. I could hardly wait to get out of sooty, noisy Chicago to open land and fresh, clean air. City life was new to me.

Mr. T recommended that I consider a vacation to Arizona for a week, just for a total change. My family and I had met missionaries to the Navajos, so I pursued that as a possibility and wrote to the Perraults. They were eager to help me have a glimpse at mission work and offered a room from their empty dorm when the school was closed for vacation for a few weeks.

They suggested I take the train to Denver, then come by bus the rest of the way to Mesa Verde with its fascinating cliff dwellings. My parents had given me a wonderful book for Christmas, *America's Wonderlands* put together by the National Geographic Book Service in 1959. The book really inspired me to see everything I could about this beautiful country. I used the book to contact Mesa Verde and the Grand Canyon for places to stay while making overnight connections. The map that came with the book is still marked with the path I was able to take on this first big trip by myself.

The train ride was great, and the sleeper was perfect. I had one suitcase and a burlap container I made to hold my sketch pad and a few pieces of chalk for drawing. It was awkward, but I still had it at the end of my two-week journey.

From Denver the bus ride took me to Salida and Gunnison, where it started snowing. We held our breath as the bus makes it through the Rockies. We also went through the Black Canyon of the Gunnison, and I got off the bus at Montrose around midnight. It was dark with no one on the sidewalks. I started walking toward the tiny town center, when a police car stopped me to see if I needed help. He said he was new in town, but there was a hotel that had recently changed its name. He said he would come back in half an hour to see if I had checked into the hotel. Yes, I certainly did. The hotel I was looking for apparently had changed its name since the booking, but the policeman directed me to the hotel. Yes, there was a reservation. Phew!

The hotel was part of Colorado's history—old, fascinating transom windows that opened over the door, old plumbing, but a welcoming bed. This was my first experience with a Wild West hotel. The loud slurred speech of men and women in the hallway made me wonder what kind of a place I had selected. I could not close the transom window, but the door locked. I had a warm bath, and went to sleep soundly.

In the morning I asked where I could go for breakfast. I was directed to the bar next door in the saloon. Not really comfy with being in a saloon by myself, I was directed to a table by a man wearing holsters with guns. A red-eyed waiter took my order. I ate, paid and left. The bus arrived in about half an hour, so it was close planning.

The next leg of the trip was full of switchbacks the like of which I had never seen. We kept going until we came to the canyon at Ouray. We had to wait while a small avalanche was plowed off the road. A passenger on the bus told me that a year before a pastor driving this road with his children had been swept off the road in an avalanche. The car could not be retrieved from the valley below until the spring thaw. Not what I wanted to hear.

Not enjoying my first experience on curvy, switchback roads, I prayed that I would not get sick. I developed a headache from the higher altitude. We went through Telluride and stopped at Silverton. I was probably happier to get off that bus than anyone would have guessed!

The area was filled with folklore that boggled my mind. I began to dream of a different life full of freedom on this trip. I wanted to own a restaurant and fill it with Western antiques. I could almost see the people who would come there to eat and hear their laughter over the sound of clattering plates in the kitchen. I could see a tin cup at each place, metal service plates, swinging café doors, and windows decorated with woodbine and cactus flowers. Then I got the wildest idea of my life—I wanted a pink jeep! A desire that disappeared with reality.

The bus dropped me off at Mesa Verde, right across from Durango. After checking in, I was taken to a lovely little cabin with a fire in the fireplace. It was cold, so I remember sitting by the fire, thanking the Lord for getting me to this destination. There was no way to contact the Perraults, but I was pretty sure they would come the next morning to pick me up. Unfortunately the cliff dwellings were going through some major repairs while I was there, so I could only see what was on the level ground. I enjoyed walking around observing what a cliff dwelling looked like for the first time. I don't remember eating breakfast there, but I think coffee was available.

When the Perraults arrived, they were ready for lunch, and knowing the area, they made a good choice. We headed on our way and passed Four Corners, where Utah, Colorado, New México and Arizona meet. The ride took us near Canyon de Chelly National Monument to the mission. Classes went through ninth grade at that time, I believe. A few boys stayed in the dorm because their home was so far from the school.

During my three days at the mission I found out as much as I could about their staff, their goals for the school, and the culture of the Navajos. This was my first exposure to missionary life. The Perraults managed the dormitories, serving as dorm parents for the boys and girls—their small home was in the middle. Nona had a bed ready for me in the girls' dorm.

My stomach reacted violently to the local water—something that apparently hit each person who came to Immanuel Mission. When I told Nona, she said that most visitors reacted to the water and gave me something to take to calm my upset stomach.

The teachers were in the middle of fixing things in the school, in their homes, and some had left for vacation in order to be fresh for the new year. One teacher had an incredible collection of sands from the Painted Desert—I don't recall ever seeing such bright, varied colors of sand before.

Nona said she would like me to meet one of the Christian Navajos who lived nearby. The Navajo was gracious to let me in. She had a small building with a couple of small windows, a small cooking area, and a sitting area for one or two people. Of course, I wondered how she managed. But she was used to living this way. Many of the Navajos had no concrete floor—just dirt.

One of the young students was asked to take me on a walk up the mesa and around to see the beauty of this area. It began to get dark, and I suggested he take me back down. He looked around, did not say anything, and I asked if he was lost. I think he gave me a moment of Navajo culture—look around, don't say anything, and give an outsider a scare. We had no problem getting back.

I did get a few good sketches on the trip, but it was not worth lugging the burlap bag with me. On my last evening at the school, I played some choruses for a relaxing time of singing together. Nona Perrault asked if I would be interested in looking at the first Navajo rug a new bride had made. She said that the mother-in-law was shocked that she had not made a rug and insisted that she make one. Being her first, it has some flaws, but I loved the colors: turquoise, black, white and gray. I paid $25 for it, knowing that it took this lady lots of time, making it a lovely souvenir that I still have in my home.

On my last day, the Perraults drove me to the Grand Canyon where I spent an afternoon and one day of exploring with them. We had supper together before they left. My time with them was so long ago, but I will never forget it.

There is nothing like a good look at Grand Canyon to take away your breath, especially around evening when the colors dance around in the wind. Mr. T said that since I probably would not be able to go down to look at the Colorado River, the best thing to do to appreciate the wildness of the river, I should go to the Photo Studio and see a movie by the Kolb brothers' experience with it, showing the fierce power in the Colorado River. He did not think it was expensive, but it would be very worthwhile. I quickly bought a ticket for that night, and the movie took my breath away! No longer did I think of the Colorado River as a little leak in a bucket. The speed of the river with its dangerous rocks, fallen trees, and loud roaring convinced me.

My alarm was set so I could get up in time to catch the bus for a ride back to Albuquerque where I would need to change to a bus to Denver. From Denver I had a sleeper back to Chicago. I began to count my money and went light on breakfast and lunch, beginning to worry I might not have enough for the taxi. The sleeper was wonderful. I spent the next several days thinking of this trip.

The bus went through the Painted Desert around 6 p.m., showing the most colorful sand I had ever seen. I could hardly believe what my eyes drank in as we passed through this wonderful part of God's creation. This was one of those times in my life when I wanted to capture what I saw and take it with me to enjoy forever. God must love color, because He gave us so much of it. From there we went through Winslow, the Petrified Forest, Gallup, and changed buses in Albuquerque. It was a relief to see civilization again after so many miles going through desert country. Albuquerque was a dip down into a small bowl. Nice surprise!

From there the bus went through Santa Fe, Wagon Mound, Trinidad, Walsenburg, Pueblo, Canyon City, and up to Denver. How glad I was to board my sleeper train for the night. My mind kept repeating the two-week vacation; the people, the places, and returning to IV in Chicago.

Arriving in Chicago at rush hour, I decided to take a taxi home. I asked what he would charge me to get to Thorndale. It was more than I had in my purse, so I asked him take me via the IV office so I could cash a check to pay the taxi driver.

He was not happy about my request, but agreed. It did not take long to pop inside the building, go to accounting and ask if anyone would be able to cash a small check so I could pay the taxi driver. Within half an hour we were at the brownstone below the L route on Thorndale and Kenmore. It was good to be back home, unpack and tell the girls about the trip highlights.

The next morning at work, Mr. T wanted to know how my trip was, and I relayed the highlights, thanking him for letting me have two weeks off. We talked about the stress in the office, and he said to "hang in" with him until the board met for their next meeting that summer at the Cedar Campus in Michigan.

He asked if I was willing to be dining hall hostess for the students and board members who might stay a few more days. I agreed. I looked forward to being at Cedar Campus again. But I was anxious about what the board might decide and how it would affect me.

CHAPTER 4

The Changes Begin

During my third year in the rooming house, the Chicago Board of Health made an inspection. The rumor was that more than 20 building code violations had been found. Several were health hazards. For some time water bugs had become a problem on the first floor, then the second floor. Bessie had moved to a nursing home, Eva got married, and one girl moved back to the South. That left two of us on the second floor and the girls on the third floor.

In the summer of 1964, it was time for a move. Ray and Marge Felten invited Sandy and me to join them for supper. We told them that our rooming house might be closed. They bought the house next to theirs and fixed it up for three occupants. Would we like to rent it? Yes, we would! With enthusiasm Sandy and I moved to the house on Dempster Street in Evanston, Illinois.

Three unfinished pieces of furniture that I bought and painted driftwood gray were added to my room for storage and workspace. Then Pauline or Ruth drove Sandy and me to estate sales to look for things for the rest of what we needed. We went Sunday after church, had lunch somewhere, then checked out estate sales in Evanston, Wilmette, Winnetka, Kenilworth and Glencoe, along the north shore above Chicago.

Going to estate sales helped me learn to appreciate antiques. Our Dempster house had a basement full of them. There were two player pianos, three treadle sewing machines and boxes of old tools, keys and picture frames to explore. With the Feltens' permission, I moved a treadle sewing machine up to my bedroom, refinished the wood and used it as a sewing table for my portable sewing machine. I took it with me to Washington, D.C., México City, and Quito, Ecuador, where it stayed when I returned to the U.S. years later.

The trip up to Cedar Campus, as always, took us to a beautiful place where I had gone twice before. First, I went as a college student, second, as Dr. T's personal secretary, and third, as dining room hostess, primarily.

It was after dark when I arrived with a small group. I was looking for the board secretary, and she was searching for words as she washed her hair. "Just get a good night's sleep—you will find out about any changes tomorrow." A bit ominous. I prayed. I slept eventually, trying to leave everything in God's Hands.

In the morning Charles Troutman met with me right after breakfast. He said that he had resigned as general director. The board had asked him, "In light of the reorganization of the ministry, where do you see yourself fitting in best?" To him, that was a challenge to his qualification for the job he occupied, and it became obvious that his resignation was being asked for. So he resigned quietly. Later that day, I found the man I thought was responsible for this and poured out my verbal wrath on him. When I confessed to Mr. T. what I had done, instead of being angry, as my father would have been, he leaned his head back and chuckled, saying he had already heard about it. His advice was, "Just let it go. We know that God is ultimately in control, even though we can't see it now." Good advice.

Somehow, the InterVarsity staff managed to keep going until the Urbana conference ended; then we went to a nearby mansion for a retreat. That was when things began to unravel.

The board had appointed Dr. John Alexander to replace Charles Troutman. We had an Urbana missions conference coming up after Christmas 1964, I think it was. Urbana conferences are wonderful events for college students who are seeking God's will for their lives in missions or ministry. Students meet with people who are serving God in many ways through a number of organizations and mission agencies. The attendance ran into the thousands.

Mr. T. assigned various staff to host several international speakers during the convention. He asked me to host Mr. P.T. Chandapilla from India. I counted it a privilege. Because he wore national clothing, he was fairly easy to spot in a huge crowd of people.

All the staff had not gathered together since Mr. Troutman's resignation. Because some of the Urbana guest speakers were at the retreat, too, the field staff asked for a private session with board representatives and office managers who were present. They called Mr. Troutman in for a session. Then they called in Dr. Alexander, who had been selected as the new director. Feelings ran high. I believe one thing that was accomplished was to assure the staff that the board had initiated the change. Dr. Alexander was just following God's leading in his life. Until that evening, I don't think he knew how the field staff felt. It was an awkward situation, but Mr. Troutman, always the gentleman, tried to calm everyone, saying that the board looked to the Lord for their decisions, so we needed to accept the decision they had made and move on with the work.

During the transition period, until Dr. Alexander could leave his university post and take over as president, Mr. T. worked from his home near Wheaton. I'd often take the train out to their home, bringing mail for them, and sometimes I'd take dictation to bring back to the office to transcribe. A couple of times staff brought things to me from Mr. T. It helped to have that contact.

We often just talked about what was happening and how it was in God's hands no matter what we thought or felt. Though Mr. T., Lois and their children struggled with the situation in which they found themselves, they trusted God. As a young, inexperienced secretary, I was totally unprepared for this time in my life. And as an immature Christian, I was not able to see that God was still in control.

For the next 1½ years I worked as his secretary from the office and Mr. T kept working from his home. About twice a month either I would take the train out to Wheaton, or he would send work in with someone who had met with him at his home. I kept busy, which helped. But I was very angry at God for treating his "children" this way, especially late in his career. I remember telling God that He could go His way and I would take care of myself.

The personnel office talked with me about taking over the handling of gifts from donors, receipting, and thank-you letters. It was not something I would like to have done for the next 30 years, so I said I would think and pray about it. We set a deadline for me to decide; meanwhile, I was looking for work elsewhere. The more I looked for work, the more angry I got that Mr. T and I both had to change our lives. I did not think anything I did would not be that enjoyable for long. So I handed in my resignation and started looking for jobs through someone recommended by a friend at church in Evanston.

Mr. T recommended that I spend a weekend at Bear Trap Ranch in the mountains near Colorado Springs. He said that a fabulous, large Navajo rug had been given to the guest cabin. I was to be a guest of the ranch for two days; then I moved into the women's dorm for the last two days there. Mr. T had my itinerary and had asked someone to meet me at the bus stop in Colorado Springs. A young staffer met me and drove me up the mountains to the ranch where I stayed in the guest cabin for a few days between camps. (That was very kind, indeed.) The first night I had a horrible bout of altitude sickness (9,400 feet) and was thankful I was not in a dorm. By the next morning I was OK again. Back then, Colorado Springs looked like a town out of a Western movie. When I moved to Colorado Springs years later, I did not recognize anything except the Broadmoor Hotel.

While I was at the ranch, one of the staff asked if I would go to the bus station and pick up a staff worker coming for the next camp. I had the choice of a car with a clutch that kept popping into neutral or a car with bad brakes. I chose the one with the clutch problem. I took the steep Old Stage Road down past the Will Rogers Shrine high above the Broadmoor Hotel, but my impression was that the other road simply had to be better. After I picked up the staff member, we returned to the ranch on Gold Camp Road. If I had known how narrow that road was, and how close to the edge it was, I think I'd have returned the way I came.

Campers arrived at Bear Trap Ranch the day before I left. What a joy it was to be with them at a couple of meals together and sing hymns with them after supper. Someone in the group always had a guitar, and this group had at least two. Great music and encouraging hymns. These camps were the times when God did so much in the lives of students. It was a privilege to see the staffers in action with the students. After my long weekend at Bear Trap Ranch, someone gave me a ride back to the bus station, showing me the Garden of the Gods with its amazing huge red rocks that barely gave room for cars to go on a path all around the various structures. Years later, I would move to Colorado Springs with Reach Beyond. But I never drove back up to Bear Trap Ranch.

Time to get on the bus to go to Boulder, where the Peterson family was waiting to meet me. The babies had grown quite a bit since my last time with them in Cleveland. The first evening it began to snow and the children put on sweaters and gathered enough snow for "snow-sickles" (snow on sticks dipped in flavors). What a nice moment of relaxation.

At supper that night, I told them that I was not going to stay at IV and had no idea where to look. Chicago did not seem like home—such a huge city full of winding roads.

During that last year, I was asked to do all kinds of tasks and tedious jobs. I did everything that was asked of me, but not always with a willing heart. One of the regional directors and his family invited me come with them to their cottage in Michigan for a long weekend in May 1965. That gave me time away from the stress of the office, but I did not find the answers I searched for. The Scripture I was hanging everything on was, *"Do not be anxious about anything, but in everything, by prayer and petition, with thanksgiving, present your requests to God"* (Philippians 4:6, NIV). God did not speak in anything I could hear. No help from anywhere. Or maybe I was not listening.

The office manager was fairly new to the organization, and he wanted me to take a job that was not right for me. I was being pressed for a decision, so I knew that I would have to look for work elsewhere. This meant leaving the people who had become like family to me, and leaving a lifestyle I had found fulfilling.

CHAPTER 5

You Go Your Way, and I'll Go Mine

I'm the first to admit that the attitudes I developed were wrong, but I was hurt, angry, and I was not strong enough in my faith to see that God was still in control. My concept of Christian organizations soured. I wondered how believers in a Christian organization could treat each other in the ways I had observed. My decision was to stay as far away from Christian organizations as possible. Since it was my life, I thought I'd run it myself, and I'd ask God for help if I needed it.

The awful task of job hunting began. Back in Chicago, I checked with an agent who was looking for jobs for me. She sent me on an interview to a new, small company. The man who interviewed me swore in each sentence, to the point that it was giving me negative vibes. I got a call later in the week telling me that the job was mine if I would accept it. The next day I called back to decline the offer.

The rough edges of the non-Christian world were quite abrasive to me after three years with InterVarsity staff. My agent called with another job offer. The State Bank & Trust Co. in Evanston was looking for an assistant for the man in charge of the Investment Department. I made an appointment with the agent for a typing speed test and did well—over 60 words per minute with just one mistake. My shorthand was fast. Later that week, an appointment was set to be interviewed at the bank. I was looking forward to hearing what was involved in the job. The pay was very good, so I could go home at Thanksgiving or Christmas.

I had been a poor student in math, but because of the rebellious state I was in at this time of my life, just for the challenge of it, I accepted a job as secretary/statistician for the investment officer in a large trust department. I began work at the bank on June 21, 1965, three days after I left InterVarsity. With the promise of a new job, I told the staff at IV that I would be leaving in two weeks to take a job in Evanston, where I now lived. I thanked them for their friendship, but I was still so confused at what God had allowed, leaving me upset.

Before I left IV, I wanted to purchase all the highly valued books I could with a discount. I made a list and did purchase them. They are on my shelves here in Arizona today. The books I still have and want to keep are *Evangelism Outside the Box* by Rick Richardson, *Archeology Gives Evidence* by A. Rendle Short, and *Knowing God* by J.I. Packer. The small book on archeology has been the most helpful one to me when I began to doubt that there was a God at all.

My parents sent a sheet cake to the office for my 25th birthday on May 14. I remember they had the Wheaton College verse of the year written on the cake. It was Jeremiah 29:11 from the Emphasized Bible, Rotherham (revised), *"For I know the plans which I am planning for you, declareth Jehovah, plans of welfare, and not of calamity, To give you a future and a hope."* When I opened the box and saw the Scripture, I cried. Eric Fife's secretary gave me a hug before the others came in the kitchen. I was grateful for her understanding. A few people gave me hugs on the way out, but I was a bit numb.

I had two days to recover before I began my new job at State Bank & Trust Co. After an interview with one of the bank's employees, we went to the second floor to find out where I would work and explain what my soon-to-be-boss would expect of me. My job was to check the highs and lows of the market three times a day and record that. When someone died and had investments held in our bank, I had to evaluate the highs and lows of their investments the day before they died, the day after they died, with the day they died. Then a value could be placed on their investments.

The files were fascinating. I did not know people could invest in so many things! One client had invested in a refrigerated boxcar for a railroad company. Even just plain boxcars. Another person had made an early investment in a new company and had done extremely well with that. In one week, I had learned a lot of fascinating ways of handling money.

Quickly, I got to know the other ladies in the Trust Department and we became friends. The dress code went up, so I began to take interest in sewing jackets and skirts for the job so I could look equal to the trust they put in me.

Three ladies from different departments at the bank invited me to join them once a week for a salad lunch in a nearby neighborhood restaurant. I learned a lot from being with them—they were delightful and savvy, and I was blessed. We celebrated each secretary's birthday, and chose a very nice restaurant in the area that appealed with the best salads I ever had. We could be back to the bank within an hour. These ladies taught me a lot of life principles—not necessarily biblical ones, but good ones, nevertheless.

To get around Evanston, I bought a three-speed bicycle, and put a basket on either side of the back. No way could I afford a car. I enjoyed the exercise, except for the snow in the winter. When it was my turn to shop and cook, I loaded groceries on my bicycle and rode home. When I needed to go to the dry cleaner's or do laundry, I loaded up the baskets and biked there. During warm months, I did my laundry in the basement tubs by hand, then carried it upstairs and hung it on the clotheslines. It was so much fun, it never occurred to me that some people might have considered it a hardship. I shopped in the neighborhood grocery store and drug store, and I got to know the clerks and the pharmacist.

Missing Mom's piano at home, I inquired about renting one. It would only cost $10 a month for an upright piano. It gave our house on Dempster another piece of furniture to help fill the living room. I still had some music from my last years of piano lessons and I practiced when no one was home.

Now that we had a dining room, I invited friends for meals. When my guests felt enough at home to sit down, I felt relaxed, too. Once I prepared cherries jubilee for dessert. No matter what I did, I could not get the dessert to go up in flames. I remember calling Dad to find out what I did wrong, and he was glad to solve the problem.

While I lived here, Dad did come by with Mom on a trip to Chicago for business. He thought the house was more suitable and safe for me, than where I had lived before. He stopped resenting my leaving home.

The next several years of spiritual rebellion and quest for achievement on my own, without consulting God, did teach me many good, if hard lessons. But those "water bugs" kept me from being comfortable where I was spiritually.

During the 2½ years I worked at the bank, there was a lot to learn about stocks, bonds, trusts and probate. My job required calling a local brokerage firm three times a day to get the market highs and lows. After spending months reading *The Wall Street Journal* each day, I needed reading glasses. The work was interesting and I enjoyed the people in the bank. Once a year, each client's investments had to be given current values so they could be reviewed by my boss and a board of advisors.

Probate reports were always proofread, and I helped with that. We had "bankers hours" so each of us could work one evening a month to keep the trust department open one night a week in order that nurses and caregivers could pick up paychecks drawn from trusts. Hanging around until my report time I saw the first James Bond movie at the theater across from the bank.

My parents surprised me by sending a decorated sheet cake to the bank for my 26th birthday. It arrived in perfect shape, and there was enough to share with the whole trust department, plus two of my friends on the bank's first floor.

My parents invited me to join them and my sister Marnie for family camp at Lake Geneva. Marnie, probably around 13 then, stayed with me for a week after camp. She remembers that visit as a time when she really discovered who I was. She was only 8 years old when I left home to work in Chicago. When camp was over, I suggested Marnie spend time with me, and then we could drive to Cleveland in cousin Ann's car to attend her sister Virginia's wedding.

Marnie wanted to meet me at the bank one afternoon so we could go shopping together for some school clothes for her. I gave her directions to the bank. When she walked the two or three miles to the bank, I was proud of her. Traffic was moderate in Evanston, and the neighborhood was friendly. The time we spent together was good. When Ann's car broke down on the way to Cleveland, we ended up taking an overnight bus to Cleveland, still making it in time for the wedding.

Through my IV acquaintances I met a young man named Karl who enjoyed opera as much as I did. We decided to treat ourselves to a night at the Chicago Opera House to hear Leontyne Price sing *Aida*. Not having anything appropriate in my limited wardrobe, I made a dress for the occasion from a Vogue pattern. We took a taxi to the opera and came home on the "L" in the rain.

The music was wonderful, and Leontyne's voice was strong and clear. It was a grand evening, reminding me of the years our family business catered for the Metropolitan Opera in Cleveland. The menu went with the country of the opera. A couple of times I got to eat behind the curtains and hanging carpets where I could peek at opera patrons. If patrons could not use their opera seats, they often gave their tickets to our catering staff, my uncles or my dad. Thanks to these free tickets, I enjoyed many wonderful operas and operettas and grew to love opera and classical music.

Music always has stirred my soul, and God kept tugging at my conscience. Though my spiritual lifestyle appeared to be solid, it had become a habit of motions. My soul felt empty because of the anger in my heart encouraging the "water bugs" to hang around.

During my second year at the bank, I began to reason that if I was going to work in an office, why not do it in an interesting place—like the desert or a mining town, or better yet, overseas! It was time for another trip out West—this time taking the train to Denver, then the bus to Boulder to stay with friends from my hometown, Cleveland, Ohio.

In the process of interviewing for a job in Boulder, it was apparent that most jobs I would be interested in were government contracts. It would be necessary to become a Colorado resident in Boulder for a year to qualify for one job I thought I'd like. Apartments were available, and I found one I liked. I was even willing to work in a store like Woolworth's for a year in order to become a resident, then get a real job and buy that pink jeep.

As I was debating what to do, my hosts in Boulder introduced me to a woman at their church on Sunday who suggested that I look into the Foreign Service. That appealed to me, so when I got back to Evanston, I got an address for the Department of State and wrote for an application to work in embassies around the world. The application came, and it took a whole weekend to fill out—and a call home for information. This was a true introduction to government work—copious!

During the six months that followed, I had two interviews in Chicago. Later it became obvious that one of the interviews was with the CIA, to find out if I would be willing to work with an undercover agent, if necessary. I was told that I might not know if one of my bosses was with the CIA, but that if that were to happen, the CIA agent would *not* be my only boss.

There were Civil Service skill tests for typing and shorthand that I had to take to qualify for the job. I passed with flying colors. I had no problem with skills—just attitudes. All kinds of tests following the "yellow", the "blue", and the "red" lines at a local hospital. Results were normal.

The Feltens planned to move to Grand Rapids, so our rental house went up for sale. Time went by with no word from the Department of State, so I kept working at the bank. Since it is easier to show a house when it is empty, I made plans to move into the Evanston Inn, at that time owned by Senator Charles H. Percy.

My brother David borrowed a company Econoline van, drove from Cleveland to Evanston, and loaded the vehicle. That night it was beastly hot, but he slept on the sofa, got up early in the morning and drove back to Cleveland. After three months at the inn, the bank pressed me for a departure date. Finally, I picked a November date out of the air and stuck to it. Just before Thanksgiving, I left my job at the bank and went back to Cleveland to wait for a call from the Department of State.

I returned home to the guest room again. This was a busy time in our family business, so I did whatever needed to be done to earn money. I waited on tables at catering functions, folded boxes, made hors d'oeuvres, drew graphs for accounting, sat by cash boxes at catering events, and helped in the order department.

Months went by with no word from Washington, D.C., because there was a hiring freeze at the Department of State until May 1967. About the time my dad was beginning to think he might be stuck with me at home forever, a call came from the Department of State telling my orders were on the way and instructing me to report for work on May 1, 1967. The call came *after* dad said I had to move out of the house. I just threw myself on God and asked for His intervention to calm my dad. But I was very sad inside, hiding it from my bakery buddies. Some more "water bugs" moved in with me at that time.

My parents did surprise me with a farewell party with some of my friends, giving me a happier departure to Washington, D.C.

Bakery office employees planned a surprise farewell party for me, as well. The staff was assembling our best canapés, hors d'oeuvres and sweets on silver platters everywhere out of sight. I returned from an errand to find a beautifully set table, silver platters of delicious food, flowers and a very fine black purse from the office staff. I was honored and humbled. Not only did it indicate that I had made a contribution to the office, but I had managed to become one of them.

It was worth the wait. After a six-month-long restriction on hiring new personnel and moving back home, I arrived in Washington, D.C., and reported to the Department of State in July 1967.

CHAPTER 6

Foreign Service, Here I Come!

Once travel orders were in my hands, I flew to Washington, D.C., reporting to the Foreign Service Institute for orientation prior to beginning an assignment as an assistant secretary in the Audit Staff.

New Foreign Service women employees stayed at the Meridian Hill Hotel on 16ᵗʰ Street while they went through orientation at the Foreign Service Institute. The hotel had a cafeteria and a small shop that sold things like newspapers, magazines, and shampoo. The neighborhood was not a safe one for single women to be alone after dark.

At the Institute, we had lectures on the importance of security, diplomacy, the damage of compromise, and the history of the Foreign Service. The Six-Day War broke out on the Golan Heights in June 1967 during my first week in Washington, D.C., and some new recruits were moved through the process of assignment quickly to go to the Middle East to fill secretarial ranks. Others were sent to Saigon, Vientiane and Bangkok. There were lots of tears.

Some girls were elated to be chosen, but others were unprepared for such an assignment. It was a time when most of us knew someone in the Vietnam War. I took my impending assignment overseas seriously, knowing I could be sent to the war zone anytime, too.

A friend from my home church was going through Marine officer training at Quantico at that time. He asked me to type a paper for him on tunnel warfare. Yes, I was glad to help, but what I learned by typing his paper put fear in my heart for him. He did survive, but lost all of his men.

Lyndon Johnson was President, and Lady Bird Johnson pushed an effort to plant a rose bush in front of every tenement and run-down home in the black community of the District to make our capital look better.

Planting a rose bush was comparable to the Dutch boy putting his finger in the hole of a dyke. It would have been laughable, except that it fueled black frustration leading to rioting, and a year later to "Tent City," with curfews in the District.

Young male college students mingled among the women in the Meridian Hill Hotel cafeteria. Some came frequently for a couple of weeks and then stopped. Several weeks later, when I was working at 18ᵗʰ and G Streets, I was surprised to see a man I recognized as one of the "students" among a group of Secret Service agents who got onto an elevator with me. The incident gave me confidence that Uncle Sam took good care of us.

After completing training time at the Foreign Service Institute, on May 14, 1967, my 27ᵗʰ birthday, in a small room with one witness, I was sworn into the U.S. Department of State Foreign Service. That informal act began the most fascinating years of my life.

I moved into a studio apartment with a borrowed folding cot. My orders allowed me to ship up to 3,000 lbs. from Cleveland, so I sent for all my belongings. I took a photograph of my stuff just after delivery—15 boxes piled up, a nail keg, and a knotty pine bookcase from a bakery store. I felt at home.

By this time, I had found a church and attended regularly. One of the young ladies who lived near me had a car and offered to pick me up each Sunday morning and night that she was in town. Since my weekends were pretty free, I offered to play the piano at church several Sunday and Wednesday nights and taught Sunday school in the fall and winter.

When an efficiency apartment was available, I said I would take it. It was on the corner of Cleveland and Ordway Street in the District—within easy walking distance to a Safeway grocery store. Standing at the kitchen sink, I could touch the stove to the left and the fridge to the right at the same time. When I walked down the hallway, I could hear bath water running and toilets flushing. For the first time in my life I had enough of my own money to buy things I needed and wanted, and I loved that independence. I enjoyed adapting.

My orders stated that I would be sent to an overseas post (such as an embassy, consulate general, or consulate) after serving a year in Washington, D.C. Until then, my assignment was secretary/stenographer with the Department of State auditors. The department was growing fast, and with the reports the auditors produced, this was the department that needed help the most. The year I was there, the department doubled the staff. It was my job to type audit reports of various posts around the world. I enjoyed it. I assisted a secretary who had been in her job for years. She wore Oxfords, and comfy, loose-fitting clothing. Her squinty eyes peeked through out-of-date glasses, and her thinning hair was about an inch long.

Part of my job was to pack supplies for the auditors to use and then send them ahead in a courier pouch. When the auditors' reports came back from overseas, if they smelled of mildew or looked moldy, I mentally ticked that place off my list of possible overseas posts. I wrote Vientiane off the list the first week.

Eventually, as the auditors got to know me, they would let me know what each post was like, and either recommend it or told me to avoid the post and why. The Foreign Service Lounge was a great place to go and check out post reports. Just the quality of a report told volumes about the post. At the back entrance of the Department of State building—the entrance most of us used—a man with a disability sold the nicest variety of flowers from a cart. I bought flowers from him often, because it was handy and the seller was worthy.

Charlie (not his real name), one of the auditors, took me out to dinner a couple of times. He was 23 years older than I was and divorced. He made work more interesting, and I liked being with someone to enjoy D.C. together. One evening he invited me to his apartment for supper. During supper, he put a photograph of his young son in front of me. If there's anything that can take a girl's appetite away, that's it! I don't remember a thing I ate, but I was glad to get home!

The director of the Audit Staff wrote in my last stateside personnel evaluation that he thought I should be encouraged to take the Foreign Service Entrance Examination. He thought I would perform well in a semi-administrative and/or management-type position in the future. I chickened out and never did take the examination because I thought secretaries would always be needed, but women taking junior-grade jobs being fast-tracked would probably be the first to be bumped in a downsizing move.

It was spring of 1968. Just when I wondered if it would ever happen, I received a post preference form to fill out. My brother Larry was in the Army Security Agency in Berlin, so I wanted to go to Germany to be near him. When I was called for my appointment with the Personnel Office, I found a wise and sympathetic counselor. I have forgotten the places I chose, but the regional order was the Middle East, Africa and the Far East as my three preferences. The counselor asked if I *really* wanted to go to these places for a first assignment. She said most young ladies prefer Europe for a first post. "Wouldn't you really rather go there?" I said, "Yes!"

She took her pen and crossed out my first preference, writing in "W. Germany." She said I probably would not enjoy Berlin as a first assignment but recommended Bonn, where the U.S. Embassy was at that time. I agreed, and she wrote "Bonn." She also talked me out of my second and third choices. She knew how urgently vacancies at the embassy in Bonn needed to be filled at that time, so we never discussed any other place.

It was just a short time after our meeting that I received authorization to go to Bonn, Federal Republic of Germany in May 1968 to furnished quarters. As in all future orders, the last clause stated, "Tour of duty of two years, followed by home leave and transfer, subject to the needs of the service."

While I was on a last visit to Cleveland prior to going to Germany, my dad said something I'll never forget. "You can find someone who is interesting and bring him home with you. Just see that he isn't *too* interesting."

When May came, the Reflection Pool had been taken over by civil rights protesters—what we called "Tent City," and the National Guard had been called out to maintain a curfew. There were rumors that bridges connecting D.C. with surrounding areas were going to be blown up. It amazes me how few people knew about our curfew and weekend or more of total change in the District. I discovered that I could walk to work almost as quickly as using buses.

The moving and storage company said they would not be responsible for my things unless I let them come two days earlier than we had scheduled. The plan was to stay with friends in Virginia until I left for the airport, and my mom was going to meet me there. My ride came before the moving van arrived, so I asked a neighbor to let the moving company in to collect my things, then drop my key off at the front desk.

My mom and four friends saw me off at Dulles International Airport on May 30, 1968. On the flight to Frankfurt, the couple sitting next to me was from Zambia. He was a professional hunter studying for a master's degree in zoology. A whole new world was opening up to me.

My destination was Berlin for the weekend with my brother Larry. Berlin, the center of East-West conflict was a city I felt I had to see before I began work at the embassy. Larry had been stationed in Berlin for a couple of years. He was putting his degree in German to good use at a listening post for the Army Security Agency (ASA).

His friend Mike had a car and was glad to drive us around Berlin. The first place they took me to was Checkpoint Charlie at the Berlin Wall. It's hard to describe what I felt as I stood near the wall. We three just stood there quietly. The Wall was the reason all of us were in Germany. The implications were overwhelming. I checked into the Hotel Schweizerhof, then we continued our tour of West Berlin for three more hours.

The next day Larry and I traveled around Berlin by bus, then took a boat tour of the Havel River. The place where the Potsdam Agreement was signed was pointed out to us. It seemed so sad to see sailboats covering the West Berlin half of the river and lake, but no activity on the East Berlin side. The contrast of the divided city was obvious. Our boat docked at an island and we went inside a quaint restaurant that looked like a gingerbread house for a cool lemonade.

At the Berlin zoo a live band performed while people sat at tables eating or drinking under trees. Sunlight through the trees cast moving shadows on everything below. The atmosphere was reminiscent of impressionist paintings. I savored the environment and the music, closed my eyes and tried to remember it forever.

After supper, we drove around more of Berlin. I saw the new *Kongresshalle* that had been the subject of an audit the previous year where I had worked. We walked around and peered through the windows of the *Philharmonie*, home of the Berlin orchestra; then we drove through the French and British Sectors, up to

"Rubble Mountain," where Larry worked. The story is that all of the rubble left by bombings during World War II were bulldozed to this area. On top of the hill a ski jump waited for the next snow.

We stopped at the Brandenburg Gate, barricaded by concrete blocks so high the view into East Berlin was blocked. As I looked, all I could think about was President Kennedy's speech about freedom, while in my mind I heard the Brandenburg Concertos playing over and over. The tour would not have been complete without a drive down Berlin's main street, the *Kufürstendamm* (known as the *Ku'damm)*.

A vivid memory is the sight of the Kaiser Wilhelm Memorial Church with a toppled statue of the Kaiser among World War II bomb ruins of the original church. Next to it was a rebuilt modern church with beautiful blue, red and yellow stained-glass windows, reflecting life and hope felt by so many West Germans.

My third day in Berlin, Larry, a friend and I walked through the famous Tiergarten Park where an obliging swan sat on the bank of a pond near flowers so I could take its photograph. I wasn't ready to leave, but it was time to get to my assignment in Bonn. I understood more of what was at stake in keeping Berlin a viable city. That would become important in my work at the embassy.

CHAPTER 7

Working for a Legend

From Berlin I flew to Cologne and was met by a chauffeur who drove me directly to my "big sister's" apartment, where a bouquet of pink and red carnations was waiting from my new boss, Mr. Joachim von Elbe. Each new family unit was assigned a big brother or big sister to help find their way around, introduce them to people, and help arrange for U.S. government housing. Mr. von Elbe was the embassy's lawyer, attached to the Political Section, a division of about seven or eight political officers and five or six overworked secretaries.

After my bags were dropped off at an apartment, I settled in and unpacked a bit. I didn't find out until around 9 p.m. that night that I was sharing the apartment with another girl. Neither one of our assigned apartments was ready for us. It would have been helpful to know that before I spread out!

The next evening Mr. von Elbe honored me at a dinner in the Embassy Club on the Rhine River, inviting four secretaries who would be my new colleagues to be his guests. We had a window table with a view of the Rhine and watched barges chug up and down the river while we dined and the sun set. What a good beginning to two full, fascinating years in Germany.

Mr. von Elbe was the grandnephew of Felix Mendelssohn Bartholdy the composer. I believe Mr. von Elbe was 64 years old when I arrived at the embassy. Another of his distinctions was that he was the only lawyer still alive who had worked with the Allied Control Commission (high commission) after World War II, so French and British ambassadors and political counselors frequently called him to discuss treaty laws.

In 1945 at the Yalta and Potsdam Conferences, a plan was worked out by the Allies to administer and reshape Germany after World War II. Each of the four powers—Britain, the U.S., France and the Soviet Union—were assigned an occupation zone administered by military governments. Berlin was made the fifth zone, occupied by each of the same four powers. The high commission was set up to ensure unified treatment of the German population. This commission took up residence at a high point above the Rhine, almost opposite Mehlem, where the U.S. Embassy eventually was built. Bonn was still the capital of West Germany while I was there.

Mr. von Elbe, a German-born, U.S.-naturalized citizen, had left Germany during the 1930s, when it was not safe for Jews to remain. He had earned his law degrees at Harvard and Yale. A man of small stature, he was precise and gallant. I remember that he stopped his car and tipped his hat to all ladies who passed in a crosswalk. He always thought East Germans would do the right thing when it came to free access to West Germany. They never did.

Our U.S. community was called Plittersdorf. Not an inspiring name for the place, so we usually referred to our location as Bad Godesberg, the nearest town. Government housing in Plittersdorf was totally furnished except for cleaning utensils and linens. Top-ranking personnel had single homes closest to the banks of the Rhine, with extra landscaping and some curb appeal. As streets got farther away from the Rhine, apartments got smaller, and the landscaping became more sparse. Furnishing inside the homes was scaled according to the rank of the person who lived in them. Rank had privilege.

While I was becoming acquainted with my work at the embassy, I was also getting acquainted with Bonn's open market (like a farmers' market), the Kaufhof department store, the Cologne Cathedral, and the Rhine

River. A walk to the Rhine from my apartment took about 15 minutes, so I went there often. Embassy housing was in a community that flanked the west side of the Rhine. This river became my favorite place to go, think and unwind. As the swift waters flowed by, so did my thoughts and cares. It was the most wonderful thing about being in Germany, and I still miss it. I wrote a poem about what the river meant to me.

The Music of the River

When no one else around me
can understand my thoughts,
I'm glad there is a river
that makes a soothing sound.
Its laps are like the heartbeat
of a constant, certain harmony.
It accepts me as I am,
never asking questions.
At times when pressures build inside me
like a crescendo out of control,
the melody is lost.
I see my mood reflected in the river
as it swells and churns
in the turmoil of a storm.
When the river reaches flood stage,
the sound of the flute is gone,
outshouted by the roar
of the rushing, speeding river.
I only hear cymbals of demanding,
thoughtless voices clashing in my ears.
When the music reaches its pitch,
the river starts to calm,
like peace that comes
after a refreshing shower of rain.
My head clears
and perspective returns,
bringing the notes together—
endurance, patience, joy.

Again, I hear the flute,
each single instrument
that plays the melody of my life.
The river gives release
for my sad or angry feelings;
it's always there to listen
without a chiding comment,
just like a faithful friend.

On July 4 Larry came by train to Bonn for a five-day visit. It was his first trip to Bonn, though he majored in German and knew Germany well and was fluent in the language. Because of this, our travel together worked well. I had the car and the money, and Larry knew the language and the country. The Embassy Club had a barbecue for the Fourth of July. Ambassador Henry Cabot Lodge addressed the crowd at the ballpark, and we all enjoyed fireworks after dark. This was a nice change for Larry who was in the Army in Berlin.

The Rhine River and left atop the mountain is a building used during the High Commission Headquarters after WW II

The next day we took the train from Bad Godesberg to Bingen, where we boarded the Rhine River boat to ride back down the river. We saw such famous landmarks as the "Cat" and "Mouse" castles, the Lorelei (legend of the singing siren who draws sailors into the rocks), the Drachenfels, and various embassies along the Rhine.

The air was cool as we sailed in and out of sunlight, but what gorgeous views we had! Vineyards layered up the sides of hills, and Roman ruins and castle ruins were everywhere.

Sunday we heard the Bethel, Minnesota, college choir sing at the Christuskirche. I remember driving Larry back to Frankfurt to take the duty train to Berlin. I was curious about what the duty train was like. When I took the duty train months later, I wondered why I was so eager to know!

Several months after arriving in Bonn, I began to miss being with Christians. One day I met a Canadian, Eleanor, when I delivered some paperwork to the American consulate downstairs. We introduced ourselves, then she asked where I was from. When I told her I was from Cleveland, Ohio, I was amazed to discover that she knew my uncle Robbie. I discovered she was a Christian from Victoria, B.C. We had a number of friends in common. Eleanor became the strongest Christian link for me the two years I was in Bonn. Through Eleanor, I met expatriate Christians who met together for fellowship. We met in the home of a New Zealand couple active in Navigators. He was the first secretary of the New Zealand Embassy in Bonn. It's amazing how our varied backgrounds did not matter to us, and I looked forward to our worship times together until the New Zealand couple were reassigned.

Adjustments at work were amusing. The embassy telephones operated as differently as it looked. It had a dual line, and to determine if a call was on one line or the other, it was necessary to see which of the two circles had white pie-shaped pieces visible in it. I rarely got it right the first few weeks, often cutting in on my boss, who was usually talking with a foreign diplomat. That phone system was a real challenge.

The first official task I learned was how to type a telegram. It was an exacting, precise duty. I was to type an average of five telegrams a day for the next two years. Telegrams varied in length from one page to 30 or 40 pages! Many of my telegrams were more than three pages long. Each one had to be given a security classification. Most were marked "Unclassified," but some were "Limited Official Use," then there were the "Secret" telegrams, "No Distribution" telegrams (I never quite figured that out), and the "Top Secret" telegrams. Did I ever type a top-secret telegram? Yes, I did. And to this day, I don't know why it was top secret except that it referred to a document that was top secret.

My day would begin with a trip up the four-person elevator to the code room to get the incoming telegrams for my boss. The ones that were classified had a sheet of paper stapled to them denoting the classification. When I returned to my office, I'd unlock the combination padlock on my bar-lock files, pull out the long bar that it had been attached to, and flip the red and white cards to the "open" side. A secretary could get a violation or warning from one of the roving Marines if she didn't turn the sign on the filing cabinet to the right word.

I'd pull any background information for a telegram and attach it. When the mail was delivered, I'd open it, attach background files that went with any of it, and place it in order on my boss's desk. If I had a new typewriter ribbon, it had to be locked in the cabinet at night until it was impossible for the Marine guards to read. In the morning, I'd have to replace the ribbon again. Once classified information was on our desks, someone had to be present. At lunchtime, because we had a two-person suite, I would often put my boxes of work back in the filing cabinet and lock it up again. We tried to stagger our lunch hours to make it less of a hassle, but that couldn't always be arranged. The procedure became second nature quickly.

Mr. von Elbe had to send out a lot of French memos—a language I never learned. He wrote each one out for me, because I could not take dictation in a language I didn't know. I struggled through a number of those hand-typed documents with several carbon copies. I sure hated carbon copies!

Each secretary had what was called a "Burn Bag," and all carbon papers and classified sheets that were thrown away had to go in that. Oh, for a computer back then! We'd help each other out by collecting the bags from the others around us and throwing them in an incinerator. Bags were burned every day. Sometimes the Marines, who checked the embassy each night for security violations, would put our paper clips in a long chain, or type a note on our typewriter (which had to be covered each night) that said, "Almost got you." "Better luck next time." Sometimes they just drew smiley faces. They must have been bored.

Everyone took a turn as duty officer or duty secretary, being on call 24 hours a day all week long. When we added a seventh secretary in our Section, my turn came around every seven weeks. There was hardly a duty week when I wasn't called in a couple of times. There was always an incident or event in the political arena to report back to the Department of State. Our officers were good translators. Sometimes one of them would hold a newspaper and translate an entire article with ease. And in German the subject is often at the end of the sentence, so you read backwards!

All was not hard work, though. I made lots of short trips on weekends or on Saturdays during most of my two years in Germany. The architecture of the homes and buildings I passed left their imprint on my memory. A shop sign is more than informative—it is often an artistic reflection of the owner and quality of the goods inside. I was captivated by the countryside, the terraced vineyards climbing above the road, the distant castles, and the Roman ruins.

Parties kept us from getting bored during the long, gray, sunless days of winter. The first embassy party I was invited to was a cocktail party given by the head of the Political Section. He was leaving for a year at Harvard, so as was customary, he and his wife gave a party. Another couple attached to the Political Section organized a cheese and wine-tasting party with finger painting. It was informal, relaxing and even hilarious! Everyone had to come in casual dress, bring or wear an old shirt or smock, and be prepared to get messy. Everyone invited came. Among those I recall being there were my friend, Caryl Reid, the ambassador's secretary, others from the ambassador's staff, from the Administrative Section, the Economic Section and other areas of the embassy. We had a great time laughing at each other's work. It was wonderful to see our diplomats relaxed. I was surprised at the creative side of several people whose embassy roles crowded that out of their working hours. The hosts gave prizes for the best works of art that we created. For the first time we were all on equal ground.

Soon I discovered that parties were fleeting distractions, and when every party was over, I went home alone. All the social life was great for a while; then I was by myself again, struggling with the issues I kept stuffing back in my subconscious. I would deal with them another time.

The English Community Church was a disaster, mainly because the pastor was anything but Christian. His wife was living in Africa somewhere working on a doctorate. In the two years I lived in Germany, I don't remember ever seeing her. When I was not traveling, I occasionally attended the English Community Church, because it was only a mile from embassy housing. I don't remember getting anything much from the pastor's messages, but I came to realize that he had very little to give to his small congregation.

CHAPTER 8

Missing the Spiritual Connection

Larry and I both missed Christian fellowship, so after a few phone conversations, we registered for a weeklong InterVarsity retreat at Schloss Mittersill in Austria. This was my first contact with some of the people I knew who still had a connection with InterVarsity. Dr. Stan Block had been on IV's board or corporation when I worked there, and he and his family were going to Mittersill for the retreat. In fact, they came through Bad Godesberg and invited me to supper at the Bad Godesberg castle 20 minutes from my apartment. Their kindness helped bridge the gap in my spiritual walk.

Schloss Mittersill was a castle owned by International Fellowship of Evangelical Students (IFES). On Aug. 3 I took a taxi to Bad Godesberg and caught a train at 6:44 a.m. to Frankfurt to meet my brother Larry, who arrived on the duty train from Berlin.

We took a train to Munich. There we transferred to a train headed for Wörgl, where we changed to another train to take us to Kitzbühel. From Wörgl on Austrian hillsides were picturesque: neat, green, dotted with onion-style church spires and typical alpine-style homes with window boxes full of blooming geraniums and petunias.

We arrived in Mittersill too late for supper with the group, so we ate dinner in town and took a taxi to the castle. Schloss Mittersill stood on a prominent hill above the town with the same name. The pink castle was huge with walls several feet thick. Ivy-covered walls and decorative wrought iron gave the castle's age away. IFES bought the castle from Baron von Pantz, renovating it for student conferences. At one time nobility came here from around the world, including the Duke and Duchess of Windsor.

The first night I stayed in a guest room in the main part of the castle. It had a private bath, a fireplace, and one wall of beautiful knotty pine closets with black wrought-iron hardware. It seems that because I was with the embassy, the IFES staff thought I was there for vacation, rather than as part of the conference. Once the mistake was discovered, I was moved from my lovely room to a dormitory with ladies also there for the conference—among them were friends from Cherrydale Bible Church that I attended while living in Washington, D.C.

Attendees were students and IFES workers from Ghana, Peru, Jordan, the Netherlands, Switzerland, Great Britain, France, Germany, Italy, and the U.S. We ate meals together and worshiped together, and it was an uplifting experience. They had no one to play the piano for their two Sunday services, so I agreed to do it.

Monday and Tuesday were devoted to conference sessions, small discussions and meeting the other conferees. Wednesday was a free day, and someone drove a few of us to Kitzbühel to board a train for Salzburg. We walked through Salzburg, amazed at the cathedrals, then took the cable tram to the castle above the city and had lunch in the restaurant at the top. We toured the larger castle rooms and the museum of weapons, treasures, and torture instruments. It seems that most medieval castles had plenty of these three things.

Salzburg, like Berlin, drew me back to it again and again. We barely scratched the surface of all that the city had to offer in one visit. Salzburg's history is incredibly rich, making one desire to know more. It was wonderful to see the city where part of "The Sound of Music" was filmed. The Salzburg church was large, ethereal, graceful and simple.

Thursday almost all of the conferees went to Munich for the day. Construction was going on everywhere for the Olympic Games. Several of us went to see the art museum (the Alte Pinakothek) and especially enjoyed the collection of works by Rubens, Rembrandt, the van Dyke brothers, Goya, El Greco and others. I began to respect history as never before, and I began to appreciate things that outlasted their builders.

Larry and I entered the *Frauenkirke* (church) and took a winding staircase up several flights to an elevator that went to the top of the steeple, giving us a panoramic view of Munich's enormous spread of buildings as far as we could see. Later, we ate supper with some of the conferees opposite the Munich opera watching attendees in their long gowns and tuxedos during intermission.

That evening we were back at Schloss Mittersill to hear a talk on Islamic Africa. It was educational and certainly a warning of things to come. None of us could have guessed how accurate the predictions were.

On Friday, the last day of the conference, I especially enjoyed Dr. Block's talks on the Holy Spirit and tongues— something that was very pertinent at that time. Another topic was "Student Confusion and Christian Conviction," reaffirming God's standards as opposed to the new morality's inevitable failures, which we had begun to see. We had an hour of prayer for the work going on through IFES all over the world, and the conference ended.

On Saturday Larry and I left in a rush, but not before someone remembered the packages I promised to mail for him! Our experience in Munich was hilarious from beginning to end. It was suppertime, and we were competing for a table with a station full of hungry travelers. We waited in line for one restaurant for about half an hour, then we were close enough to see the menu and prices—a bit too high for our budget right then. So we went to the end of another line and were finally seated. We just had enough time to order, eat, then run for our train. I asked Larry what was on the menu, and he gave a quick translation. We ordered something that was supposed to be beef. When it came it looked grayish and tasted like musty game. Larry was eating his, so I didn't dare complain about the meat. I ate a few bites of the meat and filled up on potatoes. We both poured gravy over the meat, leaving most of it on our plates. Without a word to each other, we ate what we could, left the rest, paid the bill, got up and looked for the track to board our train to Frankfurt.

As soon as we were on the train and got settled in our compartment, Larry said, "I wonder when the dining car opens." I asked if he was still hungry. He replied, "I thought some ice cream might help get rid of the taste in my mouth." I was amazed that he had not liked the taste of the meat, either, so I started laughing. So did he. I don't believe I had ever seen Larry laugh as heartily as he did that day. We both sat there laughing for probably five solid minutes. When one of us would get composure, the other would start us off again. We both thought some ice cream might help wash down the taste from the unidentified meat.

After the announcement that the dining car was open, we left our compartment, trying not to seem too eager, and headed for the dining car. We ordered ice cream. Aah, that helped! Larry started to sneeze and sneezed with such force that he popped the top button off his shirt and it went flying in the air. When I looked up at him, I saw total dishevelment—his shirt collar was open, his clip-on tie was hanging down askew, and he was cleaning his glasses. His comment, often repeated to me in public, was "Now, don't make a scene!" I told him it was too late; he had already made one!

After we paid the bill, Larry said, "Let's walk through the dining car, go to the observation car and look around, then come back here and see if we can find my button." We spent about 15 minutes in the observation car, then came back through the dining car looking for the button. People noticed us looking on the floor to the left and right, so Larry gave me a poke and said, just keep going. I guess I was too obvious in my search.

When we arrived in Frankfurt, Larry and I spent three hours in the duty train waiting room eating wurst, reading, and meeting some Army buddies Larry worked with. I called the Blacks, a family I knew from Cherrydale Bible Church in Arlington, Virginia, to see if I could spend the night with them. Larry boarded the duty train to Berlin. The Blacks picked me up, and the next day took me to a church service in Frankfurt and a meal at the officers' club. The Blacks took me to the train station, and I arrived home with a thankful heart.

The cost of my weeklong vacation, including taxis, trains, meals, seven days at Schloss Mittersill, entrance to museums, an offering, and two books came to $132.04. Have times changed a bit?

The result of my week at Mittersill was that I was inspired to begin systematic studying of the Bible on my own. I felt that with God's help I could profit a lot from the two years in Bonn. The only problem was that I was trying to fit God into my life on my terms. I was not willing to give Him much of my time.

CHAPTER 9

Branching Out

The day came when I learned about, "other duties as assigned." Ambassador Lodge's aide needed a substitute for his vacationing secretary for one week. I was told that the ambassador had looked at the files of all the Foreign Service secretaries in the embassy and chose me for the job. My boss was pleased that I had been asked and informed me of the request. The aide I worked for that week was a bright, young Foreign Service officer. I only had one snag that week, and it was a big one. Not my fault. One day before the others returned from lunch, Ambassador Lodge asked me to come into his office for dictation, and closed the door. That immediately left the outer office area compromised, as there was no one else in the suite. Before I sat down, the ambassador was on his second sentence. I thought, "Oh, no. This is when I get the boot!" But his dictation was short enough that I caught up and was able to keep up. He signed it, and it got into the daily mail pouch.

When I left his office to type the letter, there was a flutter of activity among the staff in the outer office. "Where were you?" they asked. I explained what had happened. The consensus was, "Well, I guess we can't give the ambassador a violation, so we'll need to have two people here all the time so it won't happen again." I was off the hook and survived the week.

Mr. von Elbe was a gentleman and highly respected among the diplomatic community. One of the U.S. ambassadors to an Eastern European country came to call on Mr. von Elbe, and it was my privilege to serve them coffee in our suite. The ambassador felt so much at home that he put his feet up on the coffee table. I remarked that it was good to see one of our ambassadors able to relax. He replied, "Ah, but I'm just a very insignificant ambassador." He went on to great things.

When something went wrong at the border between East and West Germany, Mr. von Elbe was usually consulted by the French or British embassies. He always had a positive attitude, and it always disappointed him when the East Germans did not keep their word. He seemed a little sadder each time that his hope for change was not realized.

One day I heard a thumping noise near my office and went out to the hallway to investigate it. The ambassador used a private elevator from the ground to the second floor. It had gotten stuck between the first and second floor. Through the glass wall in the elevator, I saw a pair of shiny black shoes and a thumping umbrella. I went back to my office and told my boss what had happened. He said to call the Marines, so I did. A short time later the trapped ambassador had been rescued and the elevator was declared unfit. As I reflected on the ambassador's role, I wrote a poem about the experience.

The Ambassador

He steps out of his limo,
Umbrella in hand,
Prepared for a change in the weather
But hoping to change history.
His key opens the door

To a one-man elevator.
Trapped in an old design,
He's powerless, heard by few,
Stuck between the floors
Of perceived power and reality.

About every five or six weeks I would be the duty secretary on call for the Political Section. Early on a Sunday morning I was called to come in and type a press release for Governor Scranton who was on a political visit to West Germany. His aide invited me to ride in a Mercedes to the press conference at the Embassy Club. I was interested in seeing how the press release was used and listened to, leading to questions and answers. To thank me for my time, the aide treated me to coffee and brunch at the "Rathskeller," a bar and grill below the Embassy Club. I remembered the incident because it was unusual to be thanked in such a nice way.

Mary, Sherry, me, and a Marine Guard at Mr. von Elbe's retirement party

Mr. von Elbe advised me to buy a car in order to enjoy living in Europe. "One must see all of Europe he can," he'd say. "The Roman ruins, the Drachenfels, Belgium, the Netherlands, Austria—one must see it by car!" And that was true. A four-hour drive in one direction took me to the Netherlands, and a six-hour drive in another direction took me to Belgium. It was easy to see why the Allies wanted us in Germany because of the proximity to Eastern Bloc countries.

Jan, a friend and colleague in the Political Section, and I decided to create a Christmas memory together that would involve Larry. Jan and I drove to Wiesbaden right after work and stayed in the Amelia Earhart Hotel. The next morning Larry was waiting for us a the Frankfurt train station. Snow started coming down as I drove, making it hard to see the road. I drove cautiously until we got to Dinkelsbühl. Spotlights brightened up the festively decorated gingerbread architecture in this ancient town. It was a classic German Christmas.

We reached our destination of Rothenburg after dark. Rothenburg, featured in the movie, "The Brothers Grimm," is a very well-preserved, walled, 1,000-year-old city with a moat around it. Because it was not the most popular time of the year for tourists, it was a good time for us, even though the shops were all closed. Our hotel, the Eisenhut (iron hat) had a red carpet extending to the parking area. We knew it wasn't for us.

Inside the beautifully decorated lobby was a huge Christmas tree with lit candles. After changing into warmer clothing, we walked around the town. In the town square was a huge tree with white lights decorated the town square, and the *"Rathaus,"* or town hall, had seasonal trim and lights as did inns, stores and town arches. A group of men sang carols a cappella in harmony and something like a benediction that ended with "Amen." It really felt like Christmas, because my spirit was touched by the music. The Eisenhut was the only hotel ablaze with white lights outside.

The Eisenhut Hotel in Rothenburg ob der Tauber

After breakfast the next day, we walked around the town to enjoy it by daylight. An old monastery and covered wooden bridge beckoned to us. The city wall was lined with cannons. We agreed that it was a wonderful choice for the last German Christmas my friend, Jan, and brother, Larry, would have before leaving for the United States for Christmas with my family. Everything was just perfect, from the weather to the walled fortress town of Rothenburg. Because we were not paid for overtime, it was added to our vacation. Before I left Bonn, I had accumulated six weeks of compensatory (comp.) time. I needed to use my comp. time or I would lose it. I understand this was changed later, and secretaries who accumulated comp. time could be paid for it after I left the Foreign Service.

CHAPTER 10

Taking Risks but Staying Safe

Embassy colleague Jan asked me to go with her to Berlin to help her shop for a wedding dress. We decided to take the duty train I had been so curious about. That was when I found out the duty train was not comfortable—just cheap. Our compartment had six bunks, three stacked on top of each other, and I drew one of the top bunks. Because the train went through East Germany, we had specific instructions from our bosses about what *not* to do with our passports.

Larry met us at the train station in Berlin and helped us get to Harnack House (for military) thanks to Jan's connections. Larry went back to his listening post and Jan and I went to the "Ku'damm" to do some serious shopping.

While in Berlin, Jan and I wanted to take a bus tour of East Berlin. Jan was a gutsy lady, so I thought we'd be all right going together. I certainly would not have gone alone. Larry was not allowed go because of his position with the Army Security Agency. Our bosses asked us to call the American Mission in Berlin before we went to East Berlin, then call when we got back. We had agreed. We made our call to the Mission. The man at the other end of the phone was not happy with our decision, and he reinforced our need to call again when we returned from the tour. The only way he would let us go was on a bus tour, and we agreed.

East Berlin was a drab, dull, cold, impersonal, tumbledown city. There were many beautiful buildings in East Berlin, but restoration attempts barely made a dent in what needed to be done. One of the saddest things I saw was a little boy walking across the street holding his father's hand. We waved at him, and he smiled back. Then his father grabbed his arm, and with a serious look on his face, pulled the boy away from the tour bus. My thought was, "He's learning to fear right this instant."

The East Berlin waterfront was dirty and trashy, with the boats in a state of disrepair. There were very few people on the streetcars, and the cars looked filthy with dirty windows. People on the street seemed fairly well dressed—but I had been told that clothes were so expensive for East Berliners they did not have a large wardrobe.

By the time the bus got back to Checkpoint Charlie, Jan and I were so relieved to be back in free territory that we almost forgot to inform the Mission that we had returned. I was sorry to see Jan go for two reasons: I was losing a friend, and I was afraid I'd be asked to take her difficult job.

Mr. Dean, Political Counselor and the big boss, asked me to come to his office. He said he was unofficially asking if I would work for his deputy. He said, "I know he would be difficult to work for, but I would consider it a personal favor if you would take the job . . . you can say no." I thought about it for a few days, then I agreed. For one thing, from these offices you could see the Rhine River. For another, it would mean a promotion with more pay, and it was good for my service record.

I knew that quadripartite talks among the French, British, Americans and West Germans in Berlin were about to begin. The main goal of these talks was to have more access between East and West Berlin. Among the first agenda items were postal access and phone access—something that was not happening.

My new boss, Mr. Rankin (not his real name), liked the status of being served anything from coffee to a full lunch from the cafeteria. But the day that he plopped dirty dishes in his outbox on top of a document he had already signed, staining it with gravy, made me mad! My comment to him was something like, "I'm only 10 feet away from your desk, and all you have to do is ask me to remove your dishes." One morning I had my back to the door as I removed something from the file. I didn't see his coat flying through the air, and it landed on my back, falling on the floor next to me before I even realized it was airborne. Mr. Dean's secretary said to my boss, "Why didn't you just hang it up yourself?"

The talks in Berlin made a lot of extra work for everyone in the Political Section. I remember many days when I stood more than I sat. I spent a lot of time getting coffee from the top-floor restaurant for visitors and running to and from the code room. Mr. Rankin and Mr. Dean had prime offices near the Rhine River right under the offices of the ambassador and the deputy chief of the mission (DCM). In larger embassies where the ambassador might be a political appointee, the DCM makes sure things go according to policy and he takes up any slack in official entertaining, among other things. When Mr. Rankin was out of the building—and that was often—I enjoyed looking out his window at the barges going up and down the Rhine as I placed documents or messages on his desk. There was too much for me to do to linger at the window.

The embassy had an extensive motor pool of cars and drivers, and Mr. Rankin (deputy) went to the German Foreign Office frequently to talk with his counterparts there. Embassy cars had a two-way radio in them, and anyone riding in another of the fleet cars could hear all conversations that came over the system. Mr. Rankin often called from one of these cars to tell me he was on his way back to the embassy, asking me to please wait so he could dictate something. When traffic was heavy, he might call three or four times, asking me stay in the office. It often happened that once he arrived, he would say, "Why don't you go on home. It's late and I'm too tired to think clearly." Sometimes I would spend most of my day in the Berlin file vault, and I'd be ready to go home by 6 p.m. when Mr. Rankin returned prepared to work another hour or two.

One day he called me from the car and said something derogatory about the head of the U.S. Information Service, who just happened to be riding in another car and heard the comment. When the man complained, Mr. Rankin just thought it was funny. I don't know that he ever apologized. Mr. Dean was not happy about that incident which reached lots of ears in the embassy.

When the Berlin talks began, a lot of press people were in and out of the embassy. One of the reporters came to our suite to talk with either my boss or the political counselor, Mr. Dean. Because Mr. Rankin could not see the reporter sitting in the waiting area, I knew he was apt to say something he shouldn't as he burst through the double doors of our suite. As he started to say, "Boy, did they ever blow it in Berlin today!" I said, "Shh!" He said, "Don't shh me!" But it was too late. He was just about standing at the reporter's feet when he saw him.

These were the days of "détente," and there were strict guidelines about contact with diplomats from Eastern Bloc countries. Mr. Rankin went beyond the guidelines when he and his wife accepted an invitation to have dinner in the home of a Russian diplomat to see slides of their vacation in Siberia. Shortly after this, my boss decided to go sailing in the North Sea with Mr. Volga (not his real name—who was a Russian diplomat), a Finnish diplomat, and a West German. Several of us were concerned that he might have a mishap at sea, planned or accidental. This trip was a political "no-no," and I didn't expect him to return. His wife was angry about the trip and would have nothing to do with purchasing food for it. I ran into Mr. Rankin in the commissary one day before the trip. He asked, "How many cans of orange juice do you think we need for this venture?"

My reply was, "How many times a day are you going to drink orange juice?"

"Oh, I don't know. I guess I should think about that first. My wife refuses to help me with the shopping, so I'm stuck with it."

When he returned from his trip, he admitted that he nearly fell overboard into the North Sea because he was wearing the wrong kind of deck shoes.

He would often disappear during the day to play tennis with diplomats from New Zealand or Australia. He always said, "They're our best allies, you know. Got to keep up the contact!"

On the Fourth of July I was the Political Affairs duty secretary for the Political Section and Mr. Rankin asked me to check a classified document from the code room and bring it to him at the Fourth of July party given for the diplomatic community. That was definitely a "no-no!" I was not happy with this request, but I did as he asked. When I arrived at the party, he was busy talking with some Russians, so I asked someone to get his attention.

He sent word for me to go back to the embassy and wait for his call. (Meanwhile, I could have been enjoying a cheeseburger at the club.) I was annoyed at this request, feeling a bit abused, but went back to the embassy with the document. Hours went by as I waited. Finally, he called for me to meet him somewhere else near the party. I went there and waited for half an hour, but he didn't show up. By this time, I was angry enough that I went back to the party and told one of the U.S. diplomats what was going on. I said that I was going to return the document to the code room, go home and have something to eat. I had not eaten lunch or supper because of the wild goose chase I had been sent on.

My boss kept getting passed over for raises and couldn't figure it out. For a man in his position, there were only so many times that he would get passed over before his career would be stalled.

CHAPTER 11

Fairytale Castles

My brother Larry and I planned a trip to Bavaria to see King Ludwig's famous fairytale castles. We wanted to do it before he left Germany, so we chose May of 1969. I drove to Frankfurt to pick up Larry and a friend who was going our way. By 10:30 a.m. we were on the autobahn.

Larry's friend was on a three-day pass, headed for Tübingen, a famous college town near the German Chancellor's home. We walked around the town square where the *Rathaus* (town hall) was being cleaned, and then found our way up to the castle being used for university classes. From there we went down to the Neckar River to see students poling and rowing. I wish I could have recorded their energetic, harmonious singing. It was wonderful! We said goodbye to Larry's friend and headed for Füssen to see our first two castles.

It was almost dark when we arrived, but since we were so eager to see the castles, we drove until we could see them illuminated in the distance. There they were—Neuschwanstein, the fairytale castle, in spotlights high in the distance, and Hohenschwangau down near the highway. On Sunday we hiked up to Hohenschwangau to begin our touring. "Hohenschwangau," means the high swan district—a theme repeated in many of the Wittelsbach family's castles.

The Wittelsbachs still owned Hohenschwangau and used the front part of the main building when they came for a vacation and to go hunting. We walked through the rooms that are open for visitors to the castle. Wagner frequently visited King Ludwig II here. A long banquet table contained personal treasures of the Wittelsbach family from other castles that are now government-owned.

In photographs you can't see what a steep climb it is to get to Neuschwanstein. A cool rain drizzled steadily as we climbed. We were both so exhausted that we stopped talking and just walked. What a relief to reach the top of the hill! Of course, we could have taken a horse-drawn carriage, but that would have been admitting that we were both out of shape, which we were. The longer I stayed in the castle, the more curious I became about the man who designed and built it, only to live in the unfinished castle for 172 days.

Larry charted our course to see all of King Ludwig's castles and palaces. We drove to Linderhof via the Plansee—a scenic, quiet, bright-green lake, maybe because of minerals in the water. We noticed all the lakes in this area of Bavaria are the same color. The castle theme was gaudy to me: excessive rococo, and satin walls that boasted portraits of French notables such as Madame Pompadour. King Ludwig II, in fear for his life, had designed a table that was lowered to the kitchen below, where the food was put on the table, then raised to the dining room, like one he designed for Neuschwanstein. It was amazing how much creativity went into avoiding things the king feared.

As we drove away from Linderhof, I began reading a book I bought at the fairytale castle about the life of the king—something I have reread many times.

After seeing Neuschwanstein, Linderhof Castle appeared more like an elegant estate than a king's castle. Hohenschwangau Castle, where King Ludwig II was born and raised with his brother is just below the famous Neuschwanstein. One of the most unusual features is a bedroom just for Wagner when he visited Linderhof with an accurate view of the stars overhead. I have forgotten if they move according to the seasons, but it seems accurate.

May 1969 Last Trip with Larry
Germany and Austria

1   Frankfurt
2   Tübingen
3   Füssen
4   Hohenschwangau (where King Ludwig II was born and grew up)
5   Neuschwanstein
6   Garmisch-Partenkirchen
7   Herrenchiemsee
8   Munich
9   Salzburg
10 Vienna (nearby Wienerherburg, Petronell and Carnuntum)
11 Eisenstadt
12 Graz
13 Würzen Pass (the road had an 18% grade)
14 Dachau
15 Augsburg
16 Bayreuth
17 Neustadt bei Coburg
18 Würzburg
19 Rothenburg ob der Tauber
20 Worms
21 Frankfurt

Though the costs of his construction projects nearly bankrupted the kingdom at the time, today people from all around the world gravitate to Neuschwanstein to see the fairytale castle for themselves. It is massive, royal and empty.

We drove to Oberammergau and Partenkirchen where we stayed for a night. At 7 a.m. Sunday we were awakened by church bells in the belfry right across from our rooms. We found a woodcarver's shop in Garmish that was open on Sunday. Larry and I found wood carvings he would take home for Christmas for our family.

Larry did a great job of planning the trip, taking us on a path of discovery everywhere we went. I had never heard of Herrenchiemsee and had no idea why we were going to Prien am Chiemsee. Larry kept saying, "Keep your eyes peeled for a boat dock somewhere along the lake." I asked what the lake was called, and he said, "Chiemsee." We found the dock. The boat ride was our passage to Herrenchiemsee, another of Ludwig's castles. This castle had a theme of peacocks everywhere. It had a replica of the Hall of Mirrors similar to Versailles.

We continued on to Munich to see Nymphenburg Palace (construction began in 1664) as the main summer residence of former Bavarian rulers and the rulers of the Wittlesbach family. There is a Hall of Mirrors in this castle as well. The grounds are extensive with formal gardens. And as you would expect, there were white swans enjoying the beautiful lake shaded with trees on the edge of the garden.

At this point, I was on "overload," but I shall forever be grateful to Larry for our travels in Europe.

CHAPTER 12

Border Buzzing

When you are told you can't do something, you get curious about what you're missing. My brother and I were prevented from going to Eastern Europe because of our government jobs, so, naturally, it became something we wanted to get as close to the borders as we could. Larry had a friend in the military who used to flaunt the rules, hop on the train in West Berlin, ride into East Berlin and walk around just for the fun of it. But we just wanted to take a peek from a safe vantage point to see what we could on the other side of the Iron Curtain.

Larry mapped out a trip to the Czech border, the Yugoslav border, and along the East German border. He was a good navigator, keeping us on course all the time. We arrived in Salzburg, Austria, and got rooms in the Mozart Hotel for two nights. My bathroom had an unusual tub, half the length of a regular tub, but deeper and built like a chair. It looked like a bath for handicapped. I asked Larry if he had a tub like mine. He said he had been gypped! That night I discovered it was not easy for a short person to get in or out of my tub. Salzburg was a place for wonderful concerts in churches or concert halls. The gardens, the fortress above the city, the atmosphere, the history. All just wonderful!

Salzburg is synonymous with "Mozart," and we soaked in everything we could about his life and music. We had time to visit Hellbrunn (a large home of a wealthy Austrian) on the outskirts of Salzburg to see the *"Wasserspiele"* (Water Play) that Larry had visited before. Markus Sittikus, owner of Hellbrunn, had a sense of humor—his own idea of playing with water. Water fountains were put in strategic places outside to sober up guests who had too much to drink. They shot water at us when we didn't expect it—not just at the stone table and chairs. When Larry forgot one of the locations with hidden spouts, both of us got wet. And I thought he never forgot anything!

Vienna is a large metropolitan city with lots of traffic. I tried to keep my eye on the road signs as streets converged everywhere. I was driving behind a streetcar, when all of a sudden the traffic disappeared, and I was left in the path of an oncoming streetcar. Somewhere I had driven off the road. What an embarrassment! The streetcar conductor was very patient, as I backed up carefully to get out of the way.

One day in Vienna was positively not enough, and all the accommodations in the city were taken because it was Festival Week. Some 23 km from Vienna, on the road to Prague, we located the most amusing sleeping quarters that we had on the whole trip in a small, country town called Wienerherberg. The main road through town was dirt, sand and gravel, and the village looked like a ghost town. We discovered chickens in a backyard and two horse-drawn hay wagons.

A large, fairly new (but unfinished) house with a sign in English, "Rooms for Rent," caught our attention. The landlady was an ample, friendly woman who seemed quite enterprising. Her big house was unfinished, but she took us to a corner bedroom with three cots with straw mattresses and a locker for hanging clothes. After we returned late that evening, the landlady ran upstairs to our room with a light bulb in her hand. We were thankful for that! The bathtub had not been hooked up with the water supply yet, so a gallon container was there to fill the tub from the sink.

The next morning we were awakened by the sounds of a rooster crowing, chickens clucking, and hay wagons rolling by our windows. At daybreak, the other "guests" were noisily shaving, singing and laughing in the bathroom next to our room. Larry thought they were probably Czech or Hungarian laborers by the way they sang and talked. If Larry had not been with me, I would not have had the courage to stay in this place by myself.

With a giggle in my voice, I asked Larry, "Can you see Mom or Dad staying in a place like this?"

He replied, "No." Then he began laughing heartily. That got me laughing, too.

After lunch we drove to Schoenbrunn Palace for a tour, but after we had seen King Ludwig's Bavarian castles, we were disappointed. How can you top those castles? We were able to get two of the last tickets at the *"Volksoper,"* or Folk Opera to see *"Der Freischütz."* Our seats were in the second-last row of the top balcony, but the music, stage sets and costumes were absolutely outstanding. A few seats away from us, an elderly lady sang everything with the chorus, softly but audibly. Larry wondered if she might have sung with the chorus when she was younger.

During intermission, I went to the ladies' room and saw a long line. I was embarrassed as the Austrian ladies encouraged me to go to the head of the line just because I was American. Though I would have been content to wait my turn, I respected the honor they had given me and went ahead of them all. But I sure felt guilty.

When we returned to our room in Wienerherberg late that night, we discovered that the laborers were still singing, drinking and laughing in the basement. It didn't affect our sleep, and we had a good laugh about our circumstances.

Everywhere we walked in Vienna we saw horse-drawn carriages driven by men in formal attire and bowler hats. Lots of cars were decorated with flowers—all for Festival Week. This was the most popular time of the year for wonderful operas, orchestras and hundreds of people from everywhere needing hospitality during the week.

We drove to the Vienna Woods just to enjoy being there. I put a small blanket on the grass and we both stretched out under a tree. Larry had a newspaper with him, and put it over his face to keep the sun out. He began reading to me. I told him he was making it up. I said, "How can you read something that is lying across your face? No one can focus like that." Well, he proceeded to read more and more until I asked to see the newspaper myself. He was reading it indeed, but I don't know how his eyes could focus on anything that close. Was that a part of his being so very intelligent with a high IQ? Near the end of his life, he said he could not recall as much as he used to—part of aging and illness.

The next day we left Wienerherberg and drove to Petronell, the site of Carnuntum, a Roman ruin, and place where the Roman governor or head of that area used to have a beautiful, large home. Larry said that we could be sure that to keep their governors abroad happy, the Roman government would have made it as close as possible to what they would have had in Rome. Ruins of an amphitheater existed across the road from the site of the home. The Roman Empire left evidence of its civilization behind all over Europe. Every place there were ruins, I sought history books to find out what I could about what had happened there. Why couldn't history have been this much fun in school?

We drove as close to the Czech border as possible and stopped the car. Larry pointed to a building on a hill and said, "That's the palace in Bratislava." Not allowed to cross the border, we just sat in the car and looked.

Next we went to Eisenstadt where Liszt and Haydn once lived. Then we came to the breathtaking Semmering Pass and the Europa Bridge high above the road, situated in steep, beautiful forests. The pass connected Vienna with Graz, a city with Turkish influence in architecture. In Graz we joined a guided tour of a four-story building and saw armor, spears, lances, pistols, rifles, powder horns, hatchets and other weapons.

Every place we went, I noticed the things that remained after hundreds of years. And I kept wondering what would be left when I was gone.

Larry could hardly wait to begin the next step of our journey. He had selected a scenic, steeply inclined road called the "Pack Saddle," a well-named humpy, bumpy pass that would have been better for horses. He opened the sunroof of my Volkswagen and took a photograph of the city below for me. We continued along the Würtzen Pass to the Yugoslavian border where I parked a safe distance away. We watched as people crossed from one side to the other. Larry got out of the car and walked toward the border. I followed behind him. He was going to go closer to the border than I wanted him to, till I yelled for him to come back.

Dachau—how does one prepare for walking through countless photographs of the faces of those who were forced to die here? We viewed enlarged newspaper articles of the terrible atrocities that took place here and in other death camps. We did not go to the crematorium. Larry would have gone, but it was hot, around 2 p.m., and I was feeling faint from the overwhelming horror of the photographs smuggled out of the camps, the heat of the day, and hunger. I just couldn't go there.

A Jewish couple lived next to us in University Heights, Ohio. One day the neighbor told my mother that her grandchildren, a boy and girl, were coming with their uncle to live with them for a while. I looked forward to having someone to play with, but when they came I saw faces that were sad and serious, just like little adults. They didn't seem to want to play, and I didn't understand it. Then Mom told me their story.

Their family was forced into a boxcar, and the parents were too ill to escape, but begged the children's uncle to save them. When the moment was right, the uncle put a child under each arm and jumped from the train. I asked Mom where the parents were now, and she said, "They were taken to a concentration camp, because they were Jewish."

Standing in the concentration camp of Dachau, Germany, I felt oppression as I remembered those two children and wondered where they were now. Had they ever gotten over their terrible childhood?

We took the autobahn to Bayreuth, where Wagner's operas are performed four weeks each summer. Then we went on to Stadtsteinach, where we spent another interesting night. We found a *"pensione"* that looked very old, parked the car, and walked under an arch to the side entrance. The innkeeper, a woman more than 50 years of age, was thrilled to have Americans in her guesthouse. She caught, killed, and deep-fried a whole chicken for us while we waited for about an hour. For the equivalent of 80 cents we each got half a chicken, a roll and a Coke.

Our rooms were on the third floor up a winding back staircase, through low doorways. The old house had settled unevenly, and my bedroom floor was so slanted that when I got out of bed the next morning and took two steps, I nearly ran into the wall. Larry's floor slanted the other way.

During breakfast the family dog, Rolf, a mongrel with straw stuck to his tail and legs, sat under our table slobbering all over Larry's hand. The dog reeked! Larry, always kind and positive said, "Just think how happy we made this woman by staying here."

After I took a photograph of the tiny hotel, as if I'd need a photo to remember it, we headed as close as we could to the East German border. At Neustadt bei Coburg, Larry and I climbed a hill to look over the border but were disappointed that misty rain obscured our view. We drove along the East German border for a while and got a creepy feeling when we noticed two rows of barbed wire and lots of signs in English warning people of their proximity to the East German border. It seemed pretty tame where we were, but from working at the embassy and in the military, we had a healthy respect for the border. We heard that at the East German border, cars were ordered to stay in a line then kept there for hours. If a driver decided to try for another line of cars, he ran the risk of being detained or starting the waiting all over again.

Coburg, the origin of the ancestors of the present British royal family, is one of the largest walled cities in Germany. Before we walked up the hill to the castle, we sat on a park bench overlooking Coburg and ate Spam and cheese sandwiches. Larry knew that this castle was the place where Martin Luther took refuge until the Diet of Worms decided his fate. As we walked around the grounds and castle, we thought of Luther's courage. Would I have had that kind of courage? Would I have been willing to go against everyone else theologically? I don't think so. A chapel here is named in Luther's honor.

Larry saved something special for me in Lichtenfels—Vierzehnheiligen—the most beautiful baroque cathedral I had ever seen. The name means "Fourteen Saints." It was uncluttered baroque with the tallest twin spires either of us had ever seen on a baroque church. Inside, white marble pillars with a slight pink tinge accented the walls, and gold trim decorated the pillars and balconies. The ceiling had three huge, beautifully painted frescoes, and the altar was bathed in light. It was really breathtaking.

Not far from Würzburg, in Dettelbach, we found the best place we stayed during the whole trip—the Grüner Baum. It had a typical *"gasthaus,"* or guesthouse atmosphere. Before supper, we explored the town's winding streets with delightful shop fronts and window boxes, ornate signs, a babbling brook and waterfall. Truly, a breath of fresh air.

We dumped our luggage in our rooms, then went down to the dining area for supper where we ordered Serbian steak. It was absolutely delicious and served in a warm, cozy room with red-and-green plaid tablecloths. As other guests came down, we made room around our table. Larry could speak fluent German, so he carried on meaningful conversation with the others at our table. I used what pathetic little German I could speak, and Larry interpreted for me. We felt connected with these guests, even if briefly.

The next day we left Dettelbach with a bit of regret and headed for Miltenberg. I wanted to see the town because I had bought a watercolor painting of the town square and wanted to compare it to the real thing. This picturesque old town had buildings of white stucco and timber, flower boxes filled with red geraniums, and an old town well.

We drove along the Niebelungenstrasse, an old road now paved that goes by the woods and green hills to the town of Worms.

Larry and I wanted to see the cathedral that Martin Luther made famous by posting his thesis for reform on the church door. Just a few blocks from the church there was a huge monument to Martin Luther, surrounded by statues of his friends and other reformers. Quite a change in attitude for a town over the years.

We finally arrived in Frankfurt, where I dropped Larry off to catch the duty train back to Berlin. In a rain that became a downpour, I continued on my way until I saw trucks pulling off the autobahn. I slowed down, but I was eager to get home now that I was by myself. God had given us such a good time together that I was very thankful. We had driven 2,600 miles, learned a lot and saw wonderful things, places and people.

About 18 months into my assignment in Bonn, the Department of State wanted to send me to Sofia, Bulgaria, until Mr. Dean, the political counselor, said, "Absolutely not! We need her here now that we're about to begin quadripartite talks." I had agreed to go wherever the Foreign Service needed me. To prepare for what I thought was the inevitable, I asked the Foreign Service Lounge at the Department of State to send me the post report on Sofia. When the report came, I was shocked to discover that I would have to order nearly all my foodstuffs from Vienna six months ahead of time! I could not imagine planning meals that far ahead. I would have had to get a large loan to buy a freezer and make the food purchases. At that time, it was recommended not to buy even the local pasta! When the Department of State granted Mr. Dean's request not to move me, I was greatly relieved. It went into my record that I was willing to go, and that helped me get another pay raise.

CHAPTER 13

Daughters of Mercenaries

Mary and I got talking one day about King Ludwig II of Bavaria. I loved spending time with her, because every time we talked I learned more about her background growing up in Switzerland. It was like pearl diving—one pearl or a dozen pearls, but always time well spent. I was curious about the king's paranoia. Mary said, "Well, he was afraid for his life for good reasons." She seemed so certain, that I probed for more. She did know more. She gave some examples of what she heard her grandfather talk about concerning politicians in Munich. King Ludwig II sometimes stayed in a chalet beyond her grandfather's hotel in Brunnen, Switzerland. It's probably just as well that I have forgotten everything she said, because I might be tempted to write it here.

President Nixon declared Monday, July 20, 1969, official National Moon Landing Day—the day that the men in the space capsule would walk on the moon. Mary and I decided to do something for the long weekend. She suggested that we drive to Lucerne and visit some of her relatives. I agreed. In fact, I looked forward to it.

As soon as we got to farm country in Switzerland, Mary opened the window and took a deep breath. All I could smell was cow manure. She said, "Ah, how wonderful! Swiss perfume! Can you smell it? Oh, how I've missed that smell." Her comment brought to mind the picture of a milkmaid with a cow on a chocolate bar wrapper.

The next morning we drove along the lake to Brunnen, where Mary's grandparents had owned the Grand Hotel. Her family still had an interest in the hotel at that time. As we approached Brunnen, we could see the hotel in the distance. It was a large, white hotel along a great expanse of lakefront property. The hotel was well named, "Grand." There had been cottages along the lake, below the hotel. Above it was a chalet they used for special guests. Mary's grandfather came from an old, prestigious Swiss family. During his growing-up years, her grandfather was not allowed to play anywhere near the chalet when King Ludwig II was staying there.

We drove past the hotel to the chalet where King Ludwig II had been a guest, and up to the summer cottage, where I parked the car. Mary's grandfather turned the summer cottage into an art studio for himself, with large windows for ample northern light. Even though the building was in a dilapidated state, it looked like it would have been a perfect studio for an artist.

From here Mary and I decided to take a cable car ride to the top of the hills where we could see Lake Lucerne on one side and Lake Zug on the other, just as the sun was setting. It was a beautiful sight! Some brown cows were grazing, their bells making a soft, pleasant sound.

We drove to Schwyz, the oldest town in the oldest canton of Switzerland, from which the country gets is name, Switzerland in English. While we were eating supper in a small restaurant, we noticed that there weren't too many people on the streets. Mary said that the town seemed to be deserted that evening—even the restaurant was nearly empty. She was wondering what was going on, and we were speculating about what could be happening when we commented about the lovely, full moon. "The moon!" we both said together. "Everyone's watching the moon landing!" Mary called a distant relative who lived in Schwyz, and we drove there to see the moon landing on their TV. This was the beginning of one of the most fascinating experiences of my life.

We didn't have far to go. The building was so large and the grounds so extensive, that I thought we were in front of a museum or library. As we went through an iron gate and up steps in disrepair to the front door, Mary explained that this house belonged to her three "old aunts." One never married, and the two who did eventually returned to this house. One brought her husband with her, and the other returned after her husband died. This was the old Benziger family home.

At the front door, I noticed a piece of stone was missing at the threshold. The hallway was pitch black until the maid turned a light on the staircase ahead. We went up to the second floor where the TV was already on.

We sat in a cozy room with dim light so I didn't notice right away that the maid served us tea in chipped, cracked teacups. Our attention was on the moon landing. I didn't understand the Swiss German, but Mary translated what was important. As my eyes grew accustomed to the darkness, I saw paintings on all the walls, from the chair rail almost to the ceiling. They looked like museum-quality portraits and landscapes. One of the aunts was a little more comfortable speaking English. Between the little German I knew and the English she could speak, we were able to communicate a bit. I asked about the paintings and found out they were mostly of ancestors. The landscapes were all special places to the family.

In that incredible setting, we watched the men step out of the lunar module onto the moon, bouncing around like children. What an awesome feeling I had at that moment, sitting in the past and watching the future. When the TV coverage ended, Mary and I thanked the women for letting us see this wonderful moment in history on short notice.

Mary asked one of her aunts if she would show me some of the house. She graciously agreed. On the way out of the room where we had been, I noticed some extremely old, beautiful, leather-bound books with handmade metal hasps. An "Aah!" was out of my mouth before I knew it. The aunt was pleased that I appreciated the books and unlocked a door that led us into what they called the music room. Near the entrance of the room there was a table with an architect's model of a building inset with precious and semiprecious stones and silver. When the aunt turned on more light, I saw a grand piano across the room, then the rare gilded leather adorning the walls. I had only seen such wall coverings in castles before this. The floor was beautifully inlaid with different kinds of wood in amazing patterns. It was a little shaky when we walked on it. Then I noticed paintings and heavy mirrors on the walls. A lead-crystal chandelier hung from the center of the ceiling. Mary said it was probably from Bohemia. I believe there was a Persian rug on the floor. It was a petite museum.

Back in the hallway, paintings abounded everywhere. On the way down the stairs, Mary talked with the aunt, then turned to me and said, "Oh, my, this is really something. She's going to show you the sunroom." We reached the bottom of the stairs, and the woman unlocked a door to our left, turned on a light and let us in. It was a long room full of antique furniture—exquisite antiques. There were sets of Meissen china, Oriental vases, statues, paintings stacked on the floor against the walls, Dresden china chocolate sets, dessert plates, a fur table cover, old settees, some armor and a bucket of swords in the corner. The elderly ladies were in the process of setting their house in order for their heirs. Mary pointed out a portrait of her grandmother wearing a lovely necklace with many large precious gems set in it. She said, "The sapphire in my ring came from that necklace." I was in awe. I thanked the ladies profusely for sharing their treasures with me.

The maid turned on the entrance hallway lights, and on the way out I saw that it was lined with armor and mirrors. Mary said that most of the house was closed up because of the difficulty of finding competent help in Switzerland to do housework. She also said if they would sell one of their paintings, they could probably restore the house to its original condition. But they could not part with even one of their paintings. I asked Mary where they would have acquired these treasures, and her answer surprised me. She said, "Well, they were mercenaries from way back."

Eventually, I wrote a two-page poem called, "Daughters of Mercenaries," to explain the amazing experience that way.

Daughters of Mercenaries
(Day of the Moon Walk, July 20, 1969)

Cheering voices on TV
echo through the house,
disturbing ghosts from their rest
on covered objects.
Three gray-haired sisters
sit in a darkened room
glancing at astronauts leaping on the moon
that beams on this house in Switzerland.

The first sister moves
to a massive table
and touches the cold silver
of entwined candelabra and bowls,
treasures from French kings
for battles well fought
during the Hundred Years' War.

The second sister slowly uncovers
sets of Meissen and Dresden china—
bonuses for victories at Grandson and Morat.
Drawn by a bucket of swords,
she leaves her chair
and with the sound of steel against steel,
pulls out a Turkish sword.
Tracing a red stain with her bony finger,
she remembers how Francis I regained Milan.
She swipes dangling swags of dust
from paintings on paneled walls
and Bohemian crystal chandeliers.
She tries to clean off the past.
but she and her duster are both too small.

The third sister unlocks a door
with a skeleton key.
Inside, ghosts in ballroom finery
waltz on shaky parquet,
whirling past mirrors
on gilded leather walls.
A ghost hands her a metal helmet
bearing her father's name.
She sees moonlight dancing on crossed swords,
helmets, and breastplates
mounted in the hall.
They are moving, breathing, and talking

about their conquests.
Her father's helmet gets heavier
with each battle remembered:
campaigns against the Holy Roman Empire,
the Tartars, the Hapsburgs, the Turks and the Moors.
Battles for Italy, then against it.
For Burgundy, then against it.
That moment, on the moon,
the astronauts place an American flag.

CHAPTER 14

On Duty in Berlin

Ambassador and Mrs. Lodge had left Germany and Ambassador and Mrs. Rush took their places. Ambassador Rush was appointed to the post by President Nixon. He had been an executive with Union Carbide Corporation. Shortly afterwards Caryl Reid, private secretary to Ambassador Rush for years, arrived from Union Carbide. I asked if she knew Don and Jo Parker from Union Carbide. Don had been president of one of the divisions of Union Carbide, and he and his wife had been dinner guests in our home when I was growing up. When my father asked me to play the piano for the Parkers, Jo kindly sat on the end of the bench between me and the people in the living room. Caryl knew that the Parkers were Christians, so she assumed I must be a Christian, too. We spent time together as Caryl's busy schedule would permit. I believe that at one time near the end of my two years in Bonn, I had accumulated about a month of vacation. As was the policy then, when I transferred I lost that vacation time. That was later changed to receive pay if the vacation could not be taken.

The day came when it was my turn to go to Berlin for the Political Section during the quadripartite talks. I was pleased to be asked, and when I found out that Caryl Reid was going too, that was even better. We talked about the trip; neither of us had any idea what we would be asked to do, so we tried to go prepared for anything.

We went on a military plane proudly labeled, "United States of America." It was staffed with military prepared for everything. We were instructed to be on the plane before the arrival of the French, British and U.S. ambassadors. We were all on board when Ambassador Rush and his team arrived. Next, the British ambassador arrived in a Bentley. The French ambassador was the last to arrive. The three ambassadors went to the back of the plane, where they met in a special lounge.

During the flight, we were each invited to come to the cockpit and talk with the navigator. That was when I began to understand the meaning of "flight corridors" and the importance of adhering to them, especially when flying over hostile territory. The plane had a galley that would have served almost any kind of snack or beverage we wanted.

Reservations had been made for us at the Harnack House, a small hotel for U.S. military, and chauffeurs had been assigned to each of us. I asked my chauffeur to take me to the delegation offices a little early, so that I could find out what was expected of me.

When I arrived at the offices assigned to the U.S. delegation, no one else was there. Early in my embassy service, I learned a little trick that was helpful to me many times. When I was alone in a suite, I closed the door to adjoining rooms so no one could tell if I was by myself. I had just closed the door to the conference room, when a few minutes later a man in a suit came to the door and just stood there. He looked German, but he was uncomfortable and fidgety which made me alert. I stood up, took a few steps toward the door, invited him in, looked to the left and right and couldn't see one Marine anywhere. Where were they when you needed them? The man came in and spoke English with hesitation. I understood what he said well enough to let him know that the gentleman he asked for was not there at the moment. Extending his arms, he handed me a bottle wrapped in an East German newspaper. I realized he was probably East German. I thanked him, assuring that I would deliver the gift, and he left.

My imagination went into overdrive. The first thing I tried to do was contact a Marine to make sure the bottle was not an explosive device. A Marine finally came, checked the bottle, and said it was perfectly OK.

The time came for Caryl and me to go into the room where negotiations were held. We both had paper clips, extra pens, extra notepads for things we might be asked to do, so we wouldn't get the instructions mixed with the notes. I asked for a sign when we needed to begin taking notes. Mr. Dean gave me the indication to begin. Caryl and I were both writing in shorthand as fast as we could. And we were both pretty good at it. Then I discovered that our diplomats were so used to taking notes themselves, that they were keeping right up with us. They had the advantage of knowing how everything was spelled.

After the meeting adjourned, I was taken back to the U.S. Mission and began typing my notes. Someone from our Political Section interrupted me to ask if I would type a telegram for a man who had apparently come from Washington, D.C., for the talks that day. He had begun writing notes by hand, and kept giving me pages as I typed. His expertise was Russian, and he was apparently there to interpret what the Russians had to say about the negotiations. Russians may have been present in the meetings, but I'm not certain of that. That telegram must have been close to 50 pages double-spaced. I felt sorry for the code room people! When we finished, he turned me over to one of our officers who said that I was to join Caryl Reid for dinner. A chauffeured car was available for us for the evening, because we had both done a great job that day. Caryl ordered dinner for the chauffeur and it was delivered to him in the car where he waited for us. The next day the chauffeur and car were available to us for sightseeing in Berlin. Then, just like that, it was time to return to Bonn. When I returned from Berlin I began to feel that my life was very empty. Like a child with a roomful of toys, I felt unsatisfied. Here I was, in the middle of Europe with a car, a good salary, and friends to go places with. But I was not really happy. There was no inner sense of joy that Christians are supposed to have. Whenever I bought something on my "want list" to take back to the U.S., I thought it would bring me contentment. All it gave me was a few fleeting moments of happiness. It never occurred to me that there was a spiritual problem. There were very few Christians around me, and my pride would not let me unburden my soul to any of them.

Colleagues told me that Bonn was one of the very best posts. That meant from now on it would all be downhill for me. I believed that, and it discouraged me as I thought about the future. I was in a quagmire of confusion about life and what was important.

At this low point in my life, a young couple from my home church came to Europe for a vacation. When they arrived in Bonn, we had a meal together. As we talked about spiritual things and familiar things, my body and soul were refreshed.

Mr. Dean, in charge of Political matters talked with me one afternoon about possible future posts. He said that when he had been assigned to an African post, he met missionaries there and found them to be honorable people. Missionaries were doing a marvelous job and had wonderful purpose in their lives. He said, "You might think about doing something like that, yourself. It is an honorable profession." I agreed. An honorable profession? That was definitely something to think about. And I did think about it many times in the next several years.

Caryl and I remained friends the rest of her life, stopping at her house on my many deputation trips to keep in touch with those who had given to my support account at HCJB, now called Reach Beyond. I was greatly blessed getting to know so many people during those years.

CHAPTER 15

Visit from the Home Front

Family seems especially far away when you live overseas. I looked forward to my mom and sister, Marnie, coming for a visit. The plan was to spend a couple of days with me in Bonn, then fly to Copenhagen, where Larry would join us at our friend, Jenny's (not her real name), and celebrate her birthday. Larry, Jenny and I had grown up together and attended the same church in Cleveland.

Before we flew to Copenhagen, I took Mom and Marnie to one of my favorite castles, Burg Eltz. It is just off the Moselle River and dates back to the 12th century. Because it was situated in a deep valley away from the Moselle River, there had been little damage to it, making it a great example of 12th-century architecture and painted stone floors. Another treat I had saved for their visit was lunch in Schloss Zell, a castle in the town of Zell located right on the main road along the Moselle River.

The three of us flew to Copenhagen to stay with Jenny, who worked with the CIA. While we were both working for the government in Washington, D.C., we had renewed our friendship. My parents had our own family business ship a specially decorated birthday cake to the embassy in Copenhagen for Jenny. It arrived the day after we did. It was a wonderful surprise. We enjoyed watching her face as she opened the box and found a fresh birthday cake in good condition.

Jenny was a gracious hostess, putting us up everywhere she had a couch or cot. During supper, Larry, Jenny and I told some hysterical stories from our work experiences that we had not said anything about before. Larry worked at a military facility in Berlin listening to German (his major in college). He topped the stories by telling us of a young man in his work area who never exposed his back and slid in and out of his listening post. One day some men in white attire came for him and Larry never saw him again.

The next day we took the hydrofoil to Malmö, Sweden. It was such a hot day that we went to an ice cream parlor, ordered cones and started eating them as soon as they were served. Larry went to pay for them with Danish kroner, and the lady said she could not take the kroner. I offered her German marks, but she would not take that. She said she could only take Swedish money. I offered her dollars, but she did not have change. By then we had eaten half our cones. Finally, Larry offered her American dollars again. This time she agreed to take it—probably because of our dripping cones! As we left the shop, my polite, conventional mother said, "We should have plopped the half-eaten cones down on the counter and run!"

After our time with Jenny in Copenhagen, Mom, Larry, Marnie and I flew to Berlin. This was my fourth trip to Berlin. The city, struggling for viability, fascinated me because of my work. We went to see Schloss Charlottenburg's apartments. This was the first time I was asked to wear floppy, felt slippers over my shoes to protect the floors. Because Mom's slippers were way too big for her, she kept walking out of them. We laughed so hard at her predicament that I got the hiccups. As the guide would explain something, a loud "hic" would come out of my mouth at the most inopportune moment. All I could do was smile and chew gum. We slipped, skated and slid across the floors. My hiccups lasted until the end of the tour. My family was thoroughly embarrassed. One of Larry's most important statements to me was, "Don't make a scene!" Sorry, Larry.

Back in Bonn, Mr. and Mrs. Dean (Political Section boss) invited my mother, sister and me to have Sunday dinner with them. I was pleased at this gesture of hospitality, knowing that my mother would especially appreciate meeting a man who had been so kind to me. As I recall, it was the Day of St. Francis of Assisi, and Mr. Dean read something appropriate about St. Francis at the dinner table instead of offering a prayer. During dinner the family cat climbed up the beautiful spun glass drapes in the dining room, causing quite a stir until they could get it down. My sister got a good giggle from the cat's behavior.

But that was nothing like the stir I had caused at a formal dinner in the Deans' dining room a few weeks prior. Actually, I was grateful to be invited back! Somewhere, I read that if you put perfume on the back of your knees it would give you something of a sensuous aura. So I tried it and forgot about it. The dining room table was beautifully set with fine china, crystal and silver on a beautiful wood tabletop. I was to be the dinner partner for a "visiting fireman" from the District. The meal was delicious and conversation was interesting. I was seated between the gentleman from D.C. and one of the single diplomats from the Political Section.

Suddenly, during dinner, I felt something wet lunge at my knees and let out a muffled yelp. I figured out that the dog had come into the dining room and was sniffing my knees. After a second lunge, Mr. Dean heard me and looked at me from the end of the table.

He asked, "Is everything all right down there?"

To which I replied, "Aah, I think the dog is under the table." The poor mutt was banished from the room after that.

When Mom and Marnie left, I missed them more than before they came. But I planned to go home for Christmas, just a few weeks away, on a military chartered flight. I had no idea how different the take-off timing and schedule would be going as "government" property. But saving money made it worth the many, many hours it would take.

CHAPTER 16

Stained Glass Memories

Before I left Germany for Christmas, one thing I had to have was a piece of stained glass. I admired leaded glass windows in restaurants, museums and churches and began thinking of how I could have one-foot-square folding panels made that would sit on window ledges or tabletops. Since I could not take the windows of all these places home with me, I wanted something that would be a unique reminder of these wonderful stained-glass windows.

Through friends, I found out that there was a stained glass factory not far from Bonn. One Saturday I took off for the factory. The young artisan lived above the factory with his wife and baby. As I tried to convey what I wanted in my best, but limited German, he appreciated my idea and invited me up to their home above the factory to see a stained-glass window he had made for himself. The wife graciously served me coffee while we sat and talked about the concepts I had in mind. It took every bit of German I knew to communicate well enough.

He took me back down to his workroom, and then on two long easels he mixed and matched various colors of glass. What a wonderful experience it was, choosing my own colors for two three-paneled folding screens and two lamps. I finally chose one with pale shades of aqua, mauve and amber and another with deep shades he had used for his window upstairs—emerald green, purple and blue. When I went back a couple of weeks later, I was pleased with the results. So was the young artist. In fact, the colors have come to remind me of rebuilding Germany after the war. I wrote a poem about it below:

Glassworks in Ahrweiler

His hands are cut and burned
like the Kaiser-Wilhelm
with its bombed spires and topped stone,
still smelling of smoldering ash.

He holds a paper pattern
then cuts it into pieces
like Deutschland,
hanging together from memory.

The bench is loaded with lead skeletons,
spools of solder,
piles of sawdust to cool the glass
as he melts the lead into place.

His fingers bring together
a new beginning
for the Motherland—
stained-glass windows

piece by piece—
deep blue for Maria Laach,
red for geraniums in window boxes
gold for the wise old bell in each town
and green for the banks of the Rhine.

Through my contacts at the embassy I found out that I was eligible for charter flights for military personnel from Germany to the U.S. I booked space on one of these flights and made plans to go home for Christmas. I waited in lines with dozens of other travelers and finally the lines started moving. No matter where we lined up, there were delays with no explanation. Finally, the crowd of people got on the plane, but the delays caused me to miss my connection to Cleveland. I was able to reach my parents by phone to tell them about the delay in my arrival. The weather was not good, and they needed extra time to get to the airport because I had forgotten to give them my arrival time! It seems that my brother David was the one chosen to meet me at the airport.

As the car pulled into our serpentine driveway I noticed that evergreens and a red bow decorated the post light at the end of the drive. Dad had put red and green spotlights on the front entrance. Mom decorated the house inside, and Dad decorated the house and yard outside. In the front hallway, Dad had tied the spinning wheel so it would not move, and he affixed some kind of a board to the wheel so all the Christmas cards could be tacked onto it. Coming in the front door, you would see the spinning wheel first. The house looked festive and welcoming. My folks had planned to invite lots of friends for a dinner party during the holidays. Three round tables were put in the living room, and one in the library.

One of the couples invited for supper had become good friends. The man's brother Steve (not his real name) was in town with them for the holidays, so my parents invited him too. Steve was handsome, a great dresser and had a wonderful smile. I didn't give him much thought until a letter arrived from him posted from a Cleveland suburb. We began corresponding, and by June 1970, we had made plans to see each other while I was on my home leave between assignments. The months between Christmas and June flew by! We corresponded maybe once a week with each other.

My traveling companion, Mary, and I made plans to go on a few last trips before I left Germany. My shopping list was down to good china—the biggest item. I looked at English bone china and German china, and could not find what I wanted. I liked the blue-and-white onion pattern in Meissen, but I was concerned that I might not be able to get replacement pieces someday because Meissen came from East Germany. Then in a restaurant I saw vitreous porcelain and I knew this was the pattern I wanted. I bought just one set of dishes and used them all the time for about 30 years. Little did I know when the Deutsche Mark was around four to the dollar in 1969, that someday the Villeroy & Boch dishes I picked out would become some of my most valuable possessions. I chose the Phoenix Blau pattern with a blue bird and touches of yellow and green trim. I bought 12 dinner plates, eight luncheon plates, cups, saucers, and all kinds of extra serving pieces. It was a good choice, because I have never grown tired of it, and I've cracked very few cups or saucers.

CHAPTER 17

Scottish Roots

While I was in Europe, I had a desire to meet Mom's relatives in Scotland, and I began to ask her more about her Hannah family roots. Mom was pleased to give me an address of a cousin whom she and Dad had visited when they were in Scotland a few years before. I kept the addresses and started making plans for a trip to England and Scotland.

Everything was arranged. Mary and I would drive to Belgium and take the ferry from Ostend to England, and then I'd drive a little that night to practice driving on the left side of the road. Then we'd stop for the night so I'd be fresh for concentrating on driving the next morning. For weeks I had been thinking to myself, "Think left. Think left."

Mom's cousin Margaret and her husband, George, were expecting us. They had contacted more relatives of Mom's, and it looked like I'd have a chance to meet them. If Mom's uncle was well enough, I might even be able to meet him.

We drove onto the ferry and parked the car. Walking up to the passenger level, I noticed that people were stretching out on benches everywhere. The water seemed choppy, but it was the open sea so I didn't think much of it. When it was time for supper, Mary said she wasn't hungry, but she'd go with me to the dining room and have some coffee. I ordered a meal. That was a mistake! When the food came, I suddenly realized why the dining room was empty. I felt seasick! We had a rollicking, rolling ride. Even the doors in the ladies' room would not stay in the gadget meant to hold them open. Doors were swinging, banging everywhere. It was awful!

The next morning we did the typical sightseeing all day, arriving at Ingoldsby's Guesthouse on Tor Bay after supper had been served. But, unlike the British situation comedy "Fawlty Towers," our gracious hosts cheerfully prepared and served us in the dining room. This part of England is the warmest, called the English Riviera with terraced lots decked with palm trees and tropical plants down to the sea.

When we arrived at Stratford-upon-Avon, tickets to the Royal Shakespeare Theatre had been sold out for the whole season. Instead, we toured Anne Hathaway's Cottage and walked around the town. The next day we drove to Kenilworth Castle where we walked around the ruins for an hour enjoying every minute of it. Mary knew the history of the New Coventry Cathedral. It was built right next to ruins of the original cathedral bombed during World War II. We stopped to walk through the new cathedral, enjoying the stained glass in a modern church design.

We were getting near Ripon, the area where my maternal grandfather, Alfred Warren, was born. It delighted me that it was near the Sherwood Forest, the home of Robin Hood. Mary spotted a sign that said the Old Swan Hotel was ahead. She said, "Oh, I just have to spend the night here. This would be such a treat." Remembering that Mary was from a hotel family, her reaction convinced me it probably *would* be a treat. Most of the patrons we saw looked wealthy. Yes, this was definitely going to be a treat! We watched a movie on color TV in one of the downstairs sitting rooms, and it was the best color I had seen up to 1969. The next morning Mary got up before I did, went down and paid the bill. I have no idea what the cost was for that gorgeous room with twin beds. The large bathroom had wonderful old fixtures and tiny white hexagon tiles on the floor, just like the downstairs bathroom in my paternal grandparents' home. When I asked Mary about the bill, all she would say was, "Oh, but it was such a treat! Let it be my treat. After all, you are the chauffeur and the chauffeur is worth his hire!"

The next day we drove through Brontë Country on our way to Dunblane, Scotland, where I would meet Margaret, my mother's first cousin and her husband, George. The closer we got to Dunblane, the more I realized this was near the area where my maternal grandmother, Anne Hannah Warren, grew up. We passed a sign that said "Motherwell." I remembered my grandmother talking about Motherwell. Then on the right side of the highway, I noticed thatched-roof cottages, and a sign that said "Auchenheath." That was the village where Grandma Warren was born and grew up! It looked just the same as she described it. I tried to imagine Grandma living there.

We found George and Margaret's home in a lovely area of Dunblane. Once inside, I noticed that the carpeting was red and the walls were trimmed in blue and white. I blurted out, "You must have decorated in red, white and blue just for us," not thinking that the British flag has the same colors.

George and Margaret were good-natured people with a sense of humor, and they made us feel right at home. George was a successful architect and builder. Mary noticed his Rover and asked him if he liked it, since she was thinking about buying one. Margaret had a little mini-car, and she told us that George was always after her to drive it more. So to please George, Margaret planned to drive us to Edinburgh after we returned from two days of travel further north to Inverness.

We took off for Inverness. Loch Ness was on my list of places I wanted to see, and we were intrigued by a Japanese research team parked along Loch Ness in a silver Airstream. We would have loved to have known what they were finding out about "Nessie."

We spent the night at a bed and breakfast near Fort Augustus. We drove by a narrow river and saw a sailboat go through the locks. Later, as we drove through Glen Coe, I stopped the car several times to take pictures of the waterfall and the lakes and watch the sheep. I think it was here that we rounded a corner and saw a bagpiper—just as though Kodak had put him there on a bridge over the road for that moment. We rolled the windows down and heard him play till we were too far away to hear.

Not wanting to arrive at George and Margaret's at suppertime, we first went on a tour of Doune Castle, dating back to the late 1300s. The castle was used as a hunting lodge for Scottish monarchs. There was a room above the kitchen where Mary, Queen of Scots was supposed to have stayed several times during her reign from 1542-1567. We guessed that would be the warmest room in the house and close to the kitchen. I was afraid to climb those winding, uneven, steep stone steps in the dark to see what the room was like. What a hard way of life it must have been back then. I was thankful not to have been alive when conditions were that difficult. This castle was in "tour-at-your-own-risk" condition.

Arriving at Dunblane after supper, Margaret had made trifle for dessert for us with good Scottish custard. While we ate, I asked about the Loch Ness

Margaret and Mary at Dunblane Cathedral, Scotland

Monster. They both laughed, but George did say that a friend of his claimed to have been fishing in a rowboat on Loch Ness when something like a tentacle reached up, grabbed his oar and broke it in half, leaving him with only one oar to reach the shore. He obviously made it. Other than that, they had heard things, but neither had any personal experience. They did say that the lake might have been open to the sea at one time, so any sea creatures could have been trapped in Loch Ness. That was the best information we could find, so I'm content to leave it there.

The next day Margaret drove us to Edinburgh. On the way, Margaret told us stories of the days when George courted her. They had dated for years. George did well as an architect, and eventually he bought the house they were living in. He asked Margaret to help him decorate it, and when she agreed, her family told her she was foolish to do so because he had never proposed marriage.

But then came the day George asked her, "Have ye posted yer bands, yet, Margaret?" She asked him to repeat the question.

"Have ye posted yer bands, yet, Margaret? I've had mine posted for a week now."

Grandma Warren's brother Rob with his wife

To that, Margaret said she replied, "Rrrright, George. I'll do it in the morrnin'!"

That was his proposal of marriage! The bands were the announcement of intent to marry, similar to what is done in Canada today.

Margaret took us to meet Grandma Warren's brother and sister-in-law. When I saw my grandma's brother, he looked so much like her that I was amazed. He had my Christmas picture and letter handy. I was pleased that it apparently meant so much to him that I had written to let them know I was coming for a visit, hoping to see them. He died shortly after our visit, so it was my last opportunity to meet him. Then Margaret took us to her brother's home to meet his side of the family. They fixed a lovely afternoon tea for us. Such a nice group of people! It was hard to leave them, because I wondered if I would ever see them again.

CHAPTER 18

Holland in Spring

Back in Bonn at last, Mary and I planned a last swing through Holland and Belgium before I left Germany in a few weeks. This time we took our favorite German embassy employee, Rita, as our guest. She had never been to Holland because of lack of funds, and because of an extreme dislike of the Dutch for Germans after the Second World War. Children would spit at cars going by (such as they did with mine) thinking I was German. Rita would feel more at ease being with ladies from the U.S. Embassy, so we planned a trip to Keukenhof, one of the world's largest flower gardens, when the tulips were at their peak. Rita was very excited about the trip. We chose the right weekend for the trip. The tulip beds looked like a painter's palate in every shade of the rainbow. My favorite was a pearly white tulip with a hint of pink. Landscaping made the extensive gardens seem like a collection of small outdoor rooms connected by bridges, paths and ponds.

On the way we went through the town of Delft where we toured the Royal Delft Building and watched artists hand-paint large pieces of pottery. I had seen table rugs in a showroom, so I bought three long, narrow table rugs in different colors. The rug with gold and brown tones was a Christmas present for my mother. I kept the green one. The third one must have also been a gift, but I can't recall the details.

As Dutch cities are fairly close together, we took Rita to The Hague to see the miniature village, spent a night in Utrecht, then stopped at the Kröller-Müller Museum near Apeldoorn to see a large collection of Vincent van Gogh's work. On the road from Arnhem to Tiel, we drove on a road on the top of a dike, looking at houses on one side and water on the other. It was on this road that I saw the largest hog I had ever seen. It looked like a shortened horse! I nearly swerved off the road trying to get a second look at it.

Rita wanted to thank Mary and me for the trip, so she invited us to her apartment for a typical German dinner. I'd been trying to get courage up to ask Rita about the Nazi era, so I asked what she remembered of the Second World War and the concentration camps. Her reply was that no one talked about what was going on, because they didn't know why people were disappearing. They were aware that Jews were disappearing, but so were others. She remembers that people were afraid to ask questions for fear that they would be labeled insubordinate and taken from their homes or places of work.

Living in Europe was intensely exciting for me, listening and watching as I went through the streets, stores, restaurants and public places. Even the autobahns became less hectic for me. They were like highly respected racetracks with welcome exits. My interest in modern art took a back seat, and in its place grew a fascination for old carved wood, handmade lace, crystal, Delft tiles, castles, armor, cathedrals, Roman ruins, and the Dutch masters.

I could not get enough of the Rijksmuseum in Amsterdam, the castles in Germany, or the quaint towns with their little canals in Belgium and Holland. Gradually, I gave or sold most of the several copies of Dutch masters that I purchased in the Rijksmuseum in Amsterdam. I have two copies of Vermeer's work. I also had a Pieter de Hooch that I gave away. I even bought a box of old Dutch tiles to mix with newer ones on two boards, and had them made into a nest of tables while I was living in México. My husband enjoys them next to his comfy chair for books he is reading, tea and glasses.

When the time came to request my next post in order of preference, I put San José, Costa Rica, first, because my former InterVarsity boss, Charles Troutman, and his wife were missionaries there with Latin America Mission. By now, I wanted to be where I knew I'd find Christian fellowship. When it came time to leave Bonn, the thing that made it easier was that three of us secretaries the Political Section were leaving close together. Mary would be the last one. Mr. Dean arranged a lovely dinner in a restaurant for the whole Political Section and spouses to give us a grand farewell. Our "team" was breaking up, but others would fill those holes we left behind.

Before I left Germany, I learned my next assignment would be to San José, Costa Rica! I wrote to the Troutmans to let them know I was coming. They didn't have a phone in their home, but I could call them at Latin America Mission during the day. I looked forward to being with my former boss at IV—people I knew well as I adjusted to living in a Third World culture for the first time. They were a huge support for me in my time in Costa Rica.

CHAPTER 19

I Finally Smell the Coffee

And the God of all grace, who called you to his eternal glory in Christ, after you have suffered a little while, will himself restore you and make you strong, firm and steadfast (1 Peter 5:10, NIV).

Once I was back in D.C. between assignments, the first thing I did was go to the Foreign Service Lounge to check out the post report on Costa Rica to familiarize myself with the country, what it had to offer, and what it didn't, so I could plan accordingly. Some posts allowed personnel to ship a car and some didn't. What was available varied greatly from country to country. I had a fair amount of Spanish language training, and the Department of State would provide more if I needed it. But as I looked through the post report, I saw that there was a big cultural difference between living in Germany and shopping in the commissary and living in Costa Rica, shopping in the open market. There was a small commissary in San José, but it had mostly canned goods and liquor. There was no remedy for it: I would be shopping at the market and would have to speak Spanish.

While I was home, I wanted to vacation with my family, and I wanted to see Steve. Our family liked to vacation at a place called Ipperwash Beach near Sarnia, in Ontario, Canada, and we talked about going there for one last time. Dad didn't go, but Mom, my sister and both brothers went. I remember Larry was there, because he pulled a trick on me that gave everyone at the table a good laugh. He bought a mug with an ugly frog on the bottom. When he offered to make coffee for me, he then proceeded to ask how I wanted it and even stirred the cream in, I was impressed—until I saw the frog's head. My family all smiled until I let out a yell! Mom said, "I think Larry got his money's worth out of the mug by using it once."

Steve was coming to join us for a long weekend. We met him at the Sarnia airport. At this time, Marnie was learning to drive. Steve and I took her on the same sandy roads I had learned to drive on as a teenager. She enjoyed it and was a good sport. I think she enjoyed Steve, too. Marnie is 13 years younger than I am. She used to tell me, "Have you seen the competition on the beach? Better get a new bathing suit!"

One afternoon Steve and I were sitting on the beach together. He was reading the newspaper, but I wanted to talk. I wondered if our relationship would be like this—sitting beside each other but not really communicating. We had done enough of that already. I picked up from his comments that he and his twin brother didn't go to church regularly . . . and maybe their mother didn't either. That made me uncomfortable, because I could not pinpoint his commitment as a Christian. When he left to go back to Detroit, I had an uneasy feeling about our relationship. Something was not right. I didn't know what it was, but I saw a big, red flag. I stuffed my feeling of concern and started thinking about preparing for my new assignment. Just before I left for my new post in Costa Rica, my little blue VW had to be sold, and that happened at the right moment.

The day came to fly to Costa Rica—August 6, 1970. Government employees had to fly on U.S. carriers when Uncle Sam paid the bill. My flight was on Pan American's "milk run," stopping in México City and nearly every Central American capital city. I was so glad to finally land in San José! My "big sister," assigned by the embassy to acquaint me with life in San José, made sure I knew I should not drink the water. It had to be boiled for 20 minutes. My new boss's wife knew that my last assignment was Germany, and thought I would love beer. So she filled the top shelf of the apartment-size fridge with beer. Beer was something I never liked. When I was really thirsty one day, and had no cold water for drinking, in desperation I took two swallows of beer to quench my thirst. I thought I had been poisoned! I gave away the rest of the beer. I bought a lot of soft drinks until I began boiling enough water so it would be cool when I needed it.

As I got settled in temporary housing, I noticed that the parquet floors smelled of something like kerosene. It was a bit sickening. Noisy buses went up and down the hill in front of the place where I was staying, and the black fumes were awful. Living on the local economy was the way to go, but it took time for me to recognize kinds of meat because of the way it was cut and unmarked. There was a store for chicken and a store for just pork, but that was back in 1970. It was a bit challenging after coming from Germany, but I eventually managed and learned the Spanish words for what I needed. It was a bit of culture shock adjusting, but having the Troutmans nearby really helped.

While I lived in temporary housing, I began to wheeze just as I had when I was plagued with asthma as a child. It was scary, because I thought those days were over. Someone said that perhaps living on the bus line was not a good idea. As soon as I moved into an apartment, the wheezing stopped. But I knew the asthma was still there—just latent.

My new second-floor apartment was not furnished, but the embassy had USAID furniture to loan. All I had to do was check off the items I needed on a form. The only question I was asked about furniture was whether I wanted brown, blue or green fabric. I said brown. When the furniture came, I saw several shades of brown that didn't go together well, but I covered one chair with a throw, so it didn't matter much. The big surprise was that several pieces of furniture were Ethan Allen—not their most expensive, but still!

Telephones were not easy to come-by in San José, and the embassy insisted that all of us had to have one in our home. A pleasant, retired American lady in the next apartment agreed to let me share her private line, making her phone line a party line. Every time I got on the two-person elevator, I had an uneasy feeling. I realized what it was. The elevator was lined with gray felt—like a cheap coffin.

Nearly every morning I awakened to what sounded like a woman crying. I imagined all sorts of terrible things happening to someone below me. My curiosity got so great, that I looked out a window to the courtyard below and saw a parrot squawking. There were no fast-food places yet, and meals were made fresh, from scratch. A local beauty shop gave me a permanent (the last one I ever had) with the old-fashioned curlers attached to wires. I was sure I was going to be electrocuted that day, but the treatment only burned my scalp in a couple of places. It was like stepping back 40 years to be in Costa Rica, from the kinds of cars to the things available for consumers.

Charles and Lois Troutman

When I got homesick or bored, during the three months I lived in temporary housing while I was looking for an apartment, I went by bus to visit the Troutmans. He had been my boss at IV when I was in Chicago. Through the Troutmans I met other missionaries with the Latin America Mission. I was annoyed that I had to speak Spanish outside of the embassy, but to be a good visitor in a Spanish-speaking country, it was required. I had studied Spanish for two years in high school and one year in college, but I had never learned the subjunctive verb form how to speak familiar verb tenses. Not having a car, I did very well with buses and taxis, and it forced me to speak Spanish.

There were fewer embassy functions, but embassy staff mixed more with Costa Rican local employees. Costa Rican friends had some great barbecues for several of us. It was the best of both worlds, I kept telling myself. But I was not totally comfortable in either world. Every Wednesday night I went to the Latin America Mission office for their prayer meetings. That became my spiritual food. I visited a few churches and finally settled on the one that the Troutmans attended.

My new job was in the Political Section where I was assigned as secretary to the director and his assistant. My boss and his wife had just arrived from a post in Venezuela with young children and a new baby. The baby began to be listless, so they sought medical attention. I think they had to go to Panama for a diagnosis. Apparently, the baby should have had treatment for a blood disorder at birth, but that didn't happen. The assistant was going through his own private struggle with a wife who wanted to be free. Many days they were both so wrapped up in their problems that they gave me nothing to do, so after being busy in Germany, I was very bored in Costa Rica.

Mr. Troutman (Mr. T) needed to have something typed, so I offered to bring the work to the embassy just to have something to do. A couple weeks went by before anyone noticed that I was working on something they didn't recognize. The situation was beyond the control of either of the men I worked for, but I joined the Foreign Service to work and be useful.

The only thing that kept me going was my weekly correspondence with Steve. He hadn't asked me to marry him, but we corresponded about marriage, finances, and where Steve thought we should go on our honeymoon—everything but the spiritual side of our lives was being addressed in letters.

Steve suggested that we get together the following Christmas. Since we were planning a summer honeymoon, I assumed we would announce our engagement at Christmas. So I wrote my parents how our plans were shaping in that direction. They began to plan a fancy catered engagement party for us. I told them I was thrilled, and whatever they wanted to do would be wonderful. They didn't tell me, but they had bought an engagement present—a white Italian soup tureen, something I considered the hearth of the home, a center of good times and family memories.

I told the Troutmans about my relationship, and they were pleased with the news and wanted to know more about Steve. I told them only the positive things, none of my concerns. We talked about how I could have a wedding dress made in Costa Rica for so much less, and they were encouraging. One of my embassy colleagues recommended her dressmaker who could look at a picture and duplicate anything.

Some of the gals at the embassy and I decided to spend a long weekend in Panama City so we could shop at a larger commissary. We stayed in a hotel across from a large hotel with a pool. Our plan was to enjoy as much swimming as possible. To our surprise, we discovered that the hotel across the street had no water that weekend, so the pool was full of residents who were unable to shower! Can you imagine a high-rise hotel with toilets that would not flush?

Hunting for fabric for a wedding dress, gifts for bridesmaids and my future mother-in-law was fun. A beautiful off-white lace caught my attention and I bought enough for a dress, then selected Hong Kong lace hankies for my bridesmaids, my mother and my future mother-in-law whom I had not met.

After shopping, we went to watch the ships go through the Panama Canal. I expected to see something much larger. Much later I met a woman whose father had worked on building the canal. What she told me helped me to realize that building the canal was an incredible feat. She talked about the malaria so many contracted and how many men died during construction. Yes, it was small, but the cost and benefits were huge to the country.

On the way back to Costa Rica, our flight ran into extreme turbulence. It was fall when air currents over Central America from the two oceans collide. I was so thankful to be on a Pan American airplane instead of a smaller national airline. After circling San José for a while, the pilot announced that we would fly on to Managua, Nicaragua. I was relieved that we were not going to try landing in San José.

Managua had a brand-new airport, still in the construction stages after an earthquake had destroyed the former airport. As the turbulence continued, people began praying their rosaries, crossing themselves and throwing up. The plane was like butter in a hot pan. It rolled left and right, bumped up and down. I was sure I would wake up in heaven any moment. All that went through my mind was that I was too young to die. Finally touching down in Managua, the airline crew gave us meal vouchers. Not wanting much in my stomach if we did take off again soon, I kept mine in my purse. Some of the gals in our group were hungry, so we ordered. Just as we started eating, the announcement came that there was a break in the weather over Costa Rica and our plane would take off in 15 minutes. Then, all we could think was that ordering might have been a mistake.

The whole experience was so indelible in my mind that I wrote, "Detour to Managua" sometime later.

Detour to Managua

Gray clouds veil the plane
smothering my view
and rain darts pelt the metal hulk
until droning engines only whisper.
Plastic cups roll and bounce
as the plane hits resistant air.
The sky is filled with bolts of lightning—
our plane maneuvers.
The fuselage creaks,
faces ashen.
Rosary beads come out of purses and pockets,
prayers squeeze through clammy fingers,
bead after bead.
Talking stops.
Knuckles whiten.
Quick, shallow breaths make the air warm and stuffy.
I clench my purse and think of things from Panama
thrashing around in my luggage,
things I can't buy in Costa Rica—
packaged mixes, cheddar cheese,
and Hong Kong lace for my wedding.
I would gladly give them up
just to be down—even in Managua—
no man's land since the earthquake.
Managua—moonlike except for rubble,
wooden grave markers,
and hungry dogs.

Word around the embassy was that when the weather is bad and visibility difficult, Pan Am pilots followed the Pan-American Highway into San José, because the runway was in the line of sight from there. I looked down from the plane window and saw the Pan-American Highway. Right at the end, as I had been told, was the runway. Once we landed, everyone applauded with relief!

Our mail came to an APO address in government mailbags. When the mailbags arrived, sometimes I had four letters from Steve. They were full of his plans for our honeymoon and ways he thought I should manage my money. Looking back, I think I was in love with the idea of being in love and having someone to travel with more than I was in love with Steve. The itinerary for our honeymoon was a dream! We would go to Germany, Austria, Italy, Spain, Morocco and maybe England. I could hardly wait to get back to Europe! It was going to be a perfect honeymoon, more than I ever dared hope for.

My sweet, little Scottish Grandma Warren wrote to me from her nursing home, addressing the letter to "Cassa Nova" instead of Costa Rica. That got a giggle from several friends. One day I came to work and saw several mailbags lying all over the embassy courtyard. One of the secretaries had her mother send sauerkraut for Thanksgiving, because it was part of their menu in Chicago. Two of the three glass jars broke, contaminating all the mail and smelling up the other mailbags!

Traditions! The secretary from Chicago invited several of us to have Thanksgiving in her apartment. Then she asked if I would prepare the sauerkraut. I baked it for two hours so it would be good and sour. When I arrived, I asked her to taste it. "No," she said, she didn't like it, it was just a Polish tradition. None of the rest of us had ever had sauerkraut at Thanksgiving before. So why did she ask her mother to send it? I had a bite, but most of the group passed it up.

The same colleague made an appointment for me to meet her dressmaker, and I took the beautiful lace I had bought in Panama. We discussed the basic design of my wedding dress. It was to have a straight skirt, and the lace was to cover the dress like a coat with long sleeves. He grasped the idea, took my measurements, and I left the fabric with him.

As I thought about Steve, the nagging feeling I had since our time together at Ipperwash Beach began haunting me. One day I mentioned my concern to the Troutmans and asked for their advice. Mr. T. said I should ask the Lord to stop the relationship if it was not His choice for me, then wait. I did that, but in my heart I think I knew what would happen.

All of a sudden the letters stopped. I was sure something must have happened to Steve. I talked to Mr. T. and Lois. I said if something had happened to him, I would want to know that, but if he had changed his mind, I'd want to know that, too. Mr. T. said I should call Steve. It would be the quickest way to find out what was happening. I'd know and that was better than worrying. I agreed.

When evening came, I called Steve. He answered the phone, surprised it was me and was groping for words. Immediately, I knew something had changed between us. Conversation was awkward. Steve wanted me to travel with him during the Christmas season when I came home so we could discuss our plans. I told him I couldn't do that. He agreed to call me when I got to Cleveland. At that moment, I died a little inside with the dream that was dying.

At lunchtime the next day, I went alone to a restaurant to think. I ordered something, but when it came I had the same feeling I had that first day in the Chicago rooming house. I was sick from the inside out. My heart was in my throat. I knew God had answered my prayer. It was not the answer I wanted, but I was afraid to go against God's leading in my life. This was a conscious decision to choose God's best for me. And I knew it was not to be life with Steve.

When I got home, Dad was never more understanding. In fact, he came up to the guest room where I was staying, hugged me and said, "I don't know what's wrong with these guys!" I'm sure I must have burst into tears. After all, you can only hang on so long, and sympathy opens the gate to your emotions.

My parents gave me the beautiful ivory Italian soup tureen for Christmas instead of as an engagement present. I've used it for lots of occasions and am so pleased to have it in my home today. It's a reminder of a crossroad in my life, and the engagement that wasn't to be.

That Christmas a young couple in our church got engaged. Our church had a traditional New Year's Eve service, and I went with my mother. Something that was said or prayed hit me like a ton of bricks, and I began to sob. Mom hugged me and took me out to the hallway until I could control my emotions. All I could think was that it should have been me, not that young girl showing off a diamond ring. I remember returning to Costa Rica with a heavy heart.

During the rainy season in San José, streets filled with three or four inches of water in about two hours. I always tried to catch a cab home on those days, because I ruined two pairs of shoes in these tropical downpours. From my second-floor apartment balcony, I could look down at people's backyards and see shoes sitting out where the sun could dry them and get rid of the moldy smell. Some good tablecloths that I didn't use often were getting spots of pink, blue-green and dark-brown mold. It was necessary to wash them all periodically, or air them. Ah, the tropics! Lush, green vegetation requires a price, and I was just learning how to pay it.

Susie and friend land at Playa Jaco

Three embassy secretaries beside me decided to fly to Playa Jaco (pronounced HAH-ko) with its lovely beach. The ambassador's secretary arranged for everything, even the private plane ride. The small plane took off from the airport in San José, then in about half an hour landed on the beach—a new experience at least for me. We all packed into one cabin with two double beds, changed into our bathing suits, then went to the beach. I took a long walk with Vita, the ambassador's secretary. I wanted to talk about where I was in my life, and my desire to get a transfer from Costa Rica. She was very understanding.

That night we ate freshly caught red snapper we had watched fishermen bringing from the beach. I don't think I've ever eaten more delicious, tender fish anywhere. The setting was romantic, with torches burning around the outside dining area, the sun setting on the ocean and a refreshing, gentle breeze. This was wonderfully relaxing. No phones, no work to do, nothing.

The next morning I woke up feeling sick to my stomach. Looking back, it probably was a mild case of sunstroke from too much sun the day before. Sunburned from head to foot, I thought I was going to be sick, but somehow I managed to eat something and keep it down, staying comfortable on the ride back to San José via a small plane.

The Troutmans were "comfort food" to my soul, and I spent as much time with them as I could. I needed to be busy at work, and that was still not happening. Finally, I went to the personnel officer and said I wanted a direct transfer and explained why. She said the Foreign Service head of the Latin America personnel area would be coming soon and she would mention my request. When the lady arrived, we met. She looked through some papers, then over her Benjamin Franklin reading glasses. She studied me for a moment. Her first comment to me was, "I see you have had an excellent track record with the Department. What makes you request a direct transfer at this time?" I explained my work situation and personal disappointment.

She looked at me and said, "Well, now, we can't say there is insufficient work for a secretary in the Political Section, or they won't replace you, will they."

I felt a bit of defeat, and answered, "No."

She shuffled some papers and had a quizzical frown on her face. Her next question was, "Miss Pile, are you a patient person?"

I said, "Yes, I think I am."

"Then," she said, "be patient. I have something in mind for you, but I need a couple of months."

She said it would have to be in Latin America, and most likely would be México City. (The word around the Department of State was that once you got posted to the *"cucaracha"* circuit in Latin America, you stayed there for two or three posts.)

She asked, "Can you wait that long?"

My answer was, "Yes. If there's hope of a change, I'll wait." She returned to Washington, D.C., and I waited.

She was as good as her word. Within three months I was in México City, México, assigned to the Economic Section. Though I had lived in San José only seven months from August 1970 until March 1971, my short stay had brought about a major turning point in my life.

CHAPTER 20

México City Mornings

Lunch with colleagues

In 1971 México City was huge, bustling, and a full-color sound-and-light experience. Going from one of the smallest U.S. embassies to one of the largest overwhelmed me with a bit of culture shock. México City had so many restaurants that I believe I could have eaten lunch and supper out every day for a month without repeating a restaurant. Almost anything was available, I just needed to know what it was called. I discovered that even though I could speak Spanish, the words for foods, flowers and greetings were different in México than they were in Costa Rica.

Mexican street names were impossible to pronounce on the first read-through because of all the consonants. At least I made an effort. Color was everywhere—flowers, fabric, cars, and sounds—birds, honking horns, and occasionally a mariachi band. Colorful, fragrant flowers abounded. I bought them on street corners almost every week.

My job was secretary to the deputy economic counselor—a position similar to the one I had in Germany. Most of the secretaries in the Economic Section celebrated each other's birthday with Mexican gifts. The Green Door at Cedro 8 was the best place for Mexican handmade arts and crafts. It was a warehouse of crafts and artistry in paper, glass, pottery, metal and wood.

Most days I went out for lunch or supper with a colleague. The "Zone Rosa" on the other side of Reforma Avenue from the embassy was full of restaurants of all kinds. Evenings we liked to go places where there were mariachi bands.

In spite of a very full social life, I made connection with the Capital City Baptist Church. The Lord must have worked out the details, because it was an important step in my Christian growth. I took a taxi to church and went regularly. As in Costa Rica, it was hard to get a taxi in the rain, so I bought a new VW beetle to get around. I remember driving to the *Avenida de los Insurgentes* with horrifying traffic, aiming the car straight ahead, and praying that I would avoid an accident on the way to church. Soon I offered to play piano for Wednesday-night services when they needed someone. The Kirtlands, who were with Firestone Tire Co., and the Bystroms, missionaries with the American Bible Society, reached out to me and made me part of their extended family. I had a lot of wonderful meals and encouraging fellowship in their homes. Ken Bystrom traveled a lot, so his wife Ardis and I spent many evenings together talking about life and what it meant to really live for the Lord and trust God in everything.

While still in temporary housing, I received news that my father had surgery for a brain tumor and was not doing well. The day after surgery, he began hemorrhaging and was back in surgery before I got the news through the embassy. If his life had been on the line, the Department of State would have bought me a ticket to go home immediately. I never would have expected such help. I prayed lots during those days. My father had been such a strong force in my life that I could not imagine losing him, especially now that he was "in my corner." I tried to prepare myself for the possibility.

Dad pulled through the second surgery, but it was a long couple of months before I could go home to see him. Meanwhile, I found an apartment kitty-corner to the embassy and got settled. Furniture I had left in storage in Washington, D.C., was shipped to the embassy and delivered to my apartment. Mom tried to prepare me for the change in Dad, but it was still a shock. He was no longer the strong, muscular man I knew. He had lost quite a bit of weight. When I saw him, I just smiled, hugged him and took in air, not knowing what to say.

He had finished radiation treatments the day before I came home, because he wanted to wash off the purple radiation markers on each side of his head. He achieved that goal. Dad had a tumor on the pituitary gland that pressed on the optic nerve. Doctors told us that these tumors are seldom malignant, but they are pesky because they can't be totally removed. From then on, his health went into a downward spiral—sometimes it was physical and sometimes it was mental. I was thankful to live near enough to be home in a day if necessary. Phone calls to the U.S. were cheaper from México than they had been in Costa Rica. My family needed me as much as I needed them during this time.

That fall I flew back to Cleveland for two weeks to see how Dad was doing. Finding him better, my mom and I drove to Detroit to visit her parents whom I had not seen in a while. Mom decided to take my grandparents shopping, so I could call Steve. She felt our relationship needed closure.

Steve answered the phone. He was surprised that I was in Detroit and sounded a bit relieved when I told him I was in town for a short visit with my grandparents and just wanted to say hello. For 45 minutes he described the places he visited in Europe during his summer break. It wasn't until I hung up that I realized he had gone on our honeymoon by himself! Rather than being upset, I was amused! So was my mother, when I told her about it. When we returned home, I told Dad about my conversation with Steve. It gave us all some comic relief during a stressful time. What a wonderful feeling it was to realize that I had "let go" of that relationship.

U.S. embassy from Susie's apartment

Back on the job, one of my duties was to take phone calls from Mexicans responding to invitations sent from my boss, the Economic Counselor. She loved music and had frequent open houses for music lovers and musicians. I went to many of these delightful events, usually to help with refreshments in some way. The first thing I had to learn was how to spell in Spanish. I had never been taught. So she taught me. The counselor arranged for me to join a Spanish class for 1½ hours twice a week before work with six other government employees. We discussed political cartoons and read articles from the newspaper aloud. It was excellent practice and improved my Spanish abilities. It certainly helped.

My second boss, the Deputy Director, also enjoyed music and built a harpsichord that had a prominent place in his living room. He and his wife formed a madrigal group of expatriate Americans who loved to sing. I joined the group. We sang in Latin and French (two languages I never studied). I sang French by rote. Our madrigal group got together for potluck suppers before practice times. It was a great social outlet with folk from the embassy and others in the American community. By the time Christmas came, the ambassador had heard of our group and asked us to sing in his residence.

The view each morning from my bedroom had a powerful impact on me, as I watched people two stories below line up to enter the consulate, hoping for a better life in the U.S. They started forming a line before the sun came up, even in freezing cold or rainy weather. I compared my life to the life of those who stood on the ground two floors below. Why did God choose salvation and comfort for me, when so many Mexicans were miserable and desperate to leave their country for mine? Unable to get that sight out of my mind, years later I wrote about my feeling on those México City mornings. On those cold mornings, it was so good to have a wood-burning fireplace in my living room.

México City Morning

Close together,
backs to the wind,
a line of ponchos stretches
around the American Embassy.
Warm breath turns into mist
against dark arches
and rises to the ambassador's office.

They come with mud on their shoes,
holes in their pants,
ripped-out seams.
They come with suckling children big enough to walk.
A woman pours steaming coffee from her thermos,
then passes her cup down the line.
An unshaven man in a rumpled coat
drinks from a flask.

A golden angel of independence
stands on a column of stone
with her wings outstretched.
Her skirt blows in the wind;
she inclines her head to the crowd,
but says nothing.

After house-hunting in Costa Rica and México, nightmares about the experience began to plague me. The México City apartment I chose was usually in my nightmares. Without a washer or dryer, I washed clothing in the bathtub, lugged it up two flights to the roof, then discovered how hard it was to hang sheets over wire lines without getting them dirty from the chicken wire above that helped deter thieves from stealing laundry.

One of my colleagues told me that her maid, Catalina, had one day a week free. Because she recommended her so highly, I hired her to do my laundry and some light cleaning one day a week. This was the first time I ever had a maid, and I was willing to learn how to make it work. Catalina was excellent and trustworthy.

Capital City Baptist Church desperately needed Sunday school teachers, so I agreed to teach a class of sixth- and seventh-grade girls. I enjoyed them and eventually invited them to my apartment to teach them how to make hors d'oeuvres and canapés. We made some of the things I had learned to make at home—things like "wimpies" (tiny hamburgers) with a hole in the middle made by your little finger, with ketchup in the hole, cucumber rounds, and cheese rolls. They loved it, and so did I! I didn't even mind when I discovered the girls wrote the recipes on thin 3x5 cards I gave them and some of their writing became permanently carved in my soft pine Ethan Allen coffee tables.

It rained in México City for a solid week. When the sun came out, I could see snow-capped peaks from the embassy. I had no idea they were there because of the smog obliterated them from view until after a few days of hard rain.

Since the 1940s, México City had sunk about 10-15 feet into the swamp it was built on. An old postcard showed the statue of the angel near the embassy level with the street. Now a large mound of grass existed where the city had dropped. The angel remained on the original foundation, but soil had to be built up to fill in the gap. I began noticing how the sidewalks were pulling down at an angle away from buildings. Newer buildings, more earthquake-proof did not sink as the older ones did because of their foundations built on pilings. Old postcards showed the staggering shift.

Around this time the man I had worked for was trying to straighten out the mess he made of his second marriage, hoping for a transfer back to the Department of State in D.C., and the Economic Counselor was preparing to retire to Guadalajara, México. Apparently, she wanted to give a raise to a friend with growing children to raise. So I was moved down the hall to work for one man who was hardly ever there. There were just a few months left on my assignment to México, so I would be reassigned soon. It's just the way politics works sometimes.

The U.S. Embassy had nonprofessional courier runs to the consulates. One of my colleagues had taken a mail pouch to Mérida in the Yucatán Peninsula. She encouraged me to request a trip there so I could see the pyramids of Chichén Itzá and Uxmal. My request was granted. The night before my trip, I was handed a mail pouch and told that if the plane crashed, I was to land on top of the mail pouch. I said I'd try my best.

Once in Mérida, the deputy consul came running toward me, asking if I brought the codebook. My reply was that I didn't know what was in the pouch. He took the mail pouch, relieved that he could finally decode his stacking messages. Indeed, the codebook must have been enclosed. Life is very different in a consulate or a large embassy.

The consul and his deputy were in short-sleeved shirts, without a tie or jacket in this hot climate. The consul's wife—hair in rollers—was cleaning her swimming pool at their home behind the consulate. A local (national) employee took me to meet the consul's wife, then the employee showed me around the city (a small town at best back in 1970 or 1971). The heat was incredible. We ended up in the employee's parents' home, where I met her mother and enjoyed a glass of cold lemonade. Each bedroom had metal hooks on all four walls for their hammocks to catch the best breeze. She hung her double (wedding) hammock to let me try it. As I tried to get out of it, it kept slipping underneath me. I got a wonderful dose of local culture. With my official duty done, someone dropped me off at my hotel where I took refuge from the sweltering heat in the swimming pool.

The next day I signed up for a tour to Chichén Itzá, outstanding example of Mayan civilization. Right in the middle of the guide's talk, we were pelted by a sudden, heavy, tropical rain. There was no place for shelter, so we all got soaked through to our skin. Within 30 minutes after the sun came out, we were all just as dry as we had been before the rain—wrinkled, but dry. If I had not experienced this, I would not have believed it.

Climbing at least nine or 10 stories of narrow, steep, wet, slippery stone steps inside the pyramid without a handrail, just to see the jaguar statue at the top, scared me spitless. Coming down was harder than going up. By the time I got down, I was shaking like an aspen leaf. I don't know why I ever did it. Someone told me that it is no longer open to the public inside.

After seeing the amazing Pyramid of the Magician at Uxmal, as the history books say, many questions remain unanswered.

All this time I thought I'd be able to stay in México City for two years. But one day I received a post preference form to fill out, indicating that it was time to think about moving again. The Department of State intended my stay in México City to complete the two-year term I began in Costa Rica. I decided to give my request in reverse order, putting Santiago, Chile, as my first choice; Guatemala City, Guatemala, as my second choice; and Quito, Ecuador, as my third choice. Quito was where I *wanted* to go.

When I lived in Germany I heard good things about Quito from people who had been assigned there. The guys talked about a large Christian shortwave radio station with a signal so strong that it kept cutting out baseball or football games they were trying to hear. At this point in my life, I knew I wanted to go where I'd have Christian fellowship and would be encouraged in my resolve to follow the Lord in a godly lifestyle. I was sure Quito would be that kind of a place.

Just a short time after I filed my request, I received a call from Kathy in the personnel office asking me to see her as soon as I could. Instinctively, I knew that this was going to be another direct transfer, and I knew it would be to Quito. I think the Holy Spirit was preparing my heart and mind for this new direction.

Kathy started out by saying, "I just don't understand this. This never happens! I wonder if Washington knows what they are doing."

I interrupted by saying, "It's another direct transfer, isn't it."

Kathy replied, "Yes. It is. But how did you know?"

"Is it to Quito?" I asked.

"Why, yes, it is," said Kathy.

I answered, "God prepared me for this."

Kathy proceeded to tell me that I was needed at the embassy in Quito, and in her words, "They needed you there yesterday!" She asked how soon I could be ready to leave.

"In 10 days," I replied. By then, my Hitchcock rocker would be repaired and returned.

At that time I was working in the Economic Section for two bosses—certain that one was with the "Agency," as we called it, and the other boss was a specialist in nuclear physics. The one with the "Agency" didn't want me to go and raised quite a fuss with the Deputy Chief of the Mission (DCM).

Because this boss was out of the office most of the time and gave me very little to do, I spoke to the secretary of the DCM, the No. 2 man at the embassy, about my suspicions that Mr. X was "Agency." I also spoke to my other boss, the physicist, about it. He thought I could be right. By the end of that week, Mr. X had a change of attitude and wished me well. I think Mr. X might have asked me to do five or six things during the few months I worked for him. And the Personnel Department figured I would be moved on soon, so it probably didn't matter in the whole scheme of things. But it did matter to me.

While official orders were being prepared, I began packing personal things. Several of the gals I had traveled and socialized with gave me a farewell lunch and supper. Folks at Capital City Baptist invited me into their homes for farewell meals. It was hard to leave the friendships I had made during the year in México City. The specialist in nuclear physics and his wife invited me to an elegant dinner in their home as a proper Foreign Service farewell, asking who I would like to be included in the dinner. We had a wonderful meal, gorgeous table setting, with all the crystal goblets, sterling silver tableware, chargers under the lovely china, and dessert plates to match. I was grateful to them for this gesture after only working for the specialist for maybe two months.

The key secretaries from the Economic Section of the embassy and the lovely ambassador's secretary treated me to a farewell luncheon with other friends in one of my favorite restaurants in the *Zona Rosa,* just across from the embassy.

A special privilege God gave me was to discuss spiritual matters with the nuclear physicist, talking about the faith God had granted that He was in control of even mistakes made by man that affected my life. After 1½ years in México City, I was on my way to Quito, Ecuador, high in the Andes. I knew God was ultimately in control.

CHAPTER 21

The Search Ends

Because I was sent to Quito on a direct transfer, I didn't have time to visit my family in Ohio before I left México City. It was in April 1972 when I flew Pan Am to Panama City, Panama, where I had to spend the night because of a tropical storm. Being unaccustomed to the sound of an air conditioner, the droning made it difficult to sleep, waking me up several times in the night.

The next morning, back at the Panama airport, I was sure it was a mistake when I saw I was going to board a plane with four prop engines. It was a Pan Am airplane all right, and that was encouraging, but not much! All I could think was after all the money the government had spent on me, training me, packing me up and shipping me from place to place, surely they would send me on a plane that would arrive safely in Ecuador. The only good thing about the plane was that it was so noisy that I slept soundly most of the way to Quito.

When I awoke and looked out the window, I saw Pichincha, a huge, green mountain the length of the city of Quito. It was a sight that I would enjoy every day of the 8 years that I lived there. Quito is 9,500 high, and the high altitude does not agree with everyone. The landing strip at that time was not as long as was really necessary, so there were incidents where planes went off the runway. And it was right in the middle of the city.

The personnel officer met me in the Quito airport and drove me to Hotel Colón, just a few blocks from the embassy. Quito seemed very small to me after México City. Buildings along the main road were old, with not a lot of traffic back then in 1972. The first thing I did was unpack my AM/FM radio and turn it on. To my delight I heard English! The announcer, Bob Beukema, giving a station break, "This is HCJB, the Voice of the Andes, coming to you from Quito, Ecuador." It was the Christian radio station that I heard about in Germany.

The first thing I did in any new place was walk around and observe the people, the crafts, the flowers, and look for what was unique. Crafts in México were somewhat similar to what I saw. I was feeling comfortable with Quito.

The Kirtlands in México City had given me the names of their friends in Quito: the Van Der Puys and the Springers. Looking for a church to attend on Sunday, I called John Munday, a missionary my Uncle Robbie suggested I contact. John offered to find me a ride to his Spanish-speaking church the next morning. Harry and May Yeoman picked me up at the hotel Sunday morning, and that was the beginning of the biggest change in my life. The Yeomans invited me to have lunch with them, and in the evening they took me to English Fellowship Church. There I met Joe and Betty Springer from my hometown, Cleveland, Ohio. They invited me to see a live broadcast at Radio Station HCJB, then for supper. Someone drove me back to the hotel after supper. It was a wonderful first whole day in Quito! I felt so welcomed by the HCJB family that I spent most of my free time with them during the next year.

My assignment was secretary to the embassy's administrative officer. Though I had taken some Spanish classes in México (reading the newspaper and political cartoons), I would be working more with the Spanish-speaking staff in Quito, so the embassy enrolled me in Spanish classes with a private tutor in the embassy twice a week I think it was. The young Ecuadorian tutor helped me with specific rough areas, and I learned a lot about Ecuador's recent political struggles from her. My tutor's father was in the military, and she gave me an inside view of what it was like to grow up in a military family in the country of Ecuador.

One day a young American woman, presumably a tourist, distraught about something, attempted to commit suicide in our embassy lily pond which had about 6 inches of water in it. She ran into the courtyard past the Marine guards and flopped face down in the water. The guards fished her out almost immediately, and the dripping damsel was whisked away to dry off and get some counseling. The incident made us all aware how easily someone could get inside the embassy and do some damage. Security was stepped up, and some modifications were made to the embassy entrance. It was still much more vulnerable than other embassies where I had worked, though now it is in a newer location that I have not seen. I am sure that the embassy is not so easily accessible, as I have since noticed that it is harder to enter in several countries.

Though I had picked out two apartments in Quito, the embassy didn't want me to live in either place because they were not secure enough. So I remained in Hotel Colón. We were allowed three months in temporary housing at the beginning and end of our assignments. I usually needed all of it to find a place to live that would have enough security. The weeks stretched out, and I was still in the hotel. But God used those weeks to get my full attention. I began a regular quiet time again, and I sought God's face in prayer for everything. To improve my Spanish, I even read a chapter out loud every night from the Gideon Bible in my hotel room. I had my English Bible with me. Sometimes I wondered what people in the next room had thought talking to myself.

During my many meals in the Hotel Colón restaurant, I noticed a lady with a British accent who ate alone. One day I asked if I could share her table for supper and found out her husband worked for Williams Brothers, the company building the oil pipeline from the Ecuadorian jungle to the coast. She was open to spiritual things, and she even went with me to the little church with missionaries John Munday from Canada and Mary Skinner from the UK. I had many suppers with this lady while she waited for her husband to return from the jungle.

During the night my stomach gurgled so much it kept me awake. Wondering if I had amoebas, I went to the embassy doctor. He asked what I drank at night with my meals. "A bottled soda," was my answer. He suggested that I drink hot tea instead, as the gas in the bottled drink would keep on bubbling at the high altitude. I never thought about the altitude affecting my body, but I took his advice, and it worked. At 9,500 above sea level, our bodies can react in strange ways.

Finally, the embassy agreed that I could have an apartment I liked, but insisted on my hiring a full-time maid so that the apartment would be secure. Emma was recommended to me as a good, honest worker, and though uncomfortable having someone there every day, I hired Emma. She was a single lady in her 50s, never married, with no children to support, and preferred to work 6 days a week but stay in her one-room place. I agreed. After a few weeks, we both felt more comfortable with our arrangement. Eventually, I told her she did not have to come on Saturdays and I would pay her the same amount.

When I added a dog to the household, she liked that and seemed to enjoy the dog a little too much. She prepared a main meal at noon, did the laundry, ironing, cleaning and dusting. Though she could not read or write, she remembered messages very well, and my Spanish improved as we spent time together. She made the best mushroom soup I ever ate in my life! She put the mushrooms in ice-cold water to keep them firm.

As I settled into my apartment, I started inviting HCJB friends for dinner. The embassy commissary had wonderful hams. I invited the Yeomans for a Sunday dinner of ham after church. When we all sat at the table, they were very quiet. I wondered if one of them didn't like ham. I asked Harry to say the blessing. He and May both were a bit emotional, and explained that they had given their last bit of grocery money to someone in need and had nothing except rice in their kitchen cupboard. As I recall, their monthly allowance was due the next day, so they just needed one meal that day. Their faith was a challenge and example to me.

The Foreign Service Inspection Corps made a routine visit to the embassy in Quito. Because I had helped the inspectors while they were in Costa Rica, and this was an administrative function, I was asked to work with the inspectors while they were in Quito. I received another post preference form to fill out. I remember looking at it and saying out loud, "But I don't want to go anywhere else." My life was going by in small segments that seemed very disconnected. I felt it was time to stay somewhere long enough to have deeper friendships and make a difference. As I prayed, I had no peace about another assignment elsewhere. So I waited.

Our office became a flurry of activity as we prepared for a group of Seabees who were coming to do some renovations. One of the Seabees took me out for supper after work. We found that we had a lot in common, so I took him to English Fellowship Church one Sunday night.

There were several parties for the Seabees, technically assigned to the administrative officer, my boss. We enjoyed sightseeing a couple of times, and I arranged for the men to visit Pifo and Papallacta. One night I invited the Seabees, my boss and his wife, and the Communications boss for dinner. The Seabees surprised me with an early 7th anniversary gift—two heavy brass candlesticks and a large brass compote on a pedestal bought in Riobamba, Ecuador. It was a time in my life when I was going through a spiritual battle. Before I got to spend any more time with the Seabees, they received urgent orders to go to China to construct a building for our first diplomatic overture there. As quickly as they came, they were gone.

Not wanting to continue in the Foreign Service, but not knowing what else to do, I was at a crossroad for weeks. Finally, while having a meal with the Yeomans one Sunday, I told them that I was tired of the rat race, that I didn't want to go anywhere else—I wanted to stay in Quito. When I asked them if there might be anything at Radio Station HCJB that I could do, the Yeomans replied that they had been praying that I'd be open to working with the mission. There was a great need for good secretaries, but it never occurred to me that I could be useful to the mission as a secretary. I began to consider making such a change, and I made an appointment with Dick Broach, personnel director, to discuss it. My decision was to live on savings for several months, as I was earning good money with the Department of State as a secretary.

The outcome of the meeting was that I would apply as a short-term missionary for a year to see if that was what the Lord wanted me to do. I wanted to know if I would fit into the missionary community, but I wanted to keep my foot in the door in case I decided to return to the Foreign Service. As I talked with the embassy's personnel officer, it became apparent that I would not qualify for a leave because what I was going to do was "not for the good of the service." So in faith I wrote my letter of resignation on April 10, 1973, to the Honorable William P. Rogers, Secretary of State, requesting that my resignation be accepted as of June 22, 1973. I also had to write a similar letter to the American ambassador in Ecuador.

Soon I was shocked by a letter from my Uncle Robbie with 14 reasons why I should not resign from the Foreign Service. I read through the reasons one by one and was surprised and dismayed. This was the uncle who sent birthday cards to all our denomination's missionary children. He had missionaries in his home all the time, he had visited them on the mission field, and he scheduled them to speak in our church. I went to the Yeomans with the letter, asking how to reply to my uncle. They gave me good advice. "Less is more." So I thanked my uncle for his concerns, but I let him know that I felt this was what the Lord wanted me to do; and I needed to do it now, rather than wait until I retired from the Foreign Service—one of his 14 suggestions. One of his major rejections was that my family needed me to continue in my successful career, seeing flaws in my three siblings' desire to work at something that would prosper. (Fifty years later, I now see some of his concerns in the distance, but God has provided for each of us in His grace.)

Farewell from Foreign Service

Shortly after submitting my letter of resignation, the ambassador came down to my office—a first. He said, "I don't know why you want to leave us. There should be enough heathen here to keep you busy." I could not really verbalize that yes, there were enough heathen to keep me there, neither could I disagree with him. A party was arranged for my departure, and many people encouraged me. His visit to my office was very thoughtful, and I thanked him for coming in person to express his regrets. To my surprise, the ambassador and his wife invited me, along with the financial man who was also leaving, to a farewell lunch in their home with my boss and his wife. It was my first time to eat artichoke leaves dipped in butter. Yum!

Looking back, I was getting cranky, so I am glad I proceeded with plans to make the change. I needed to sell my car or pay the taxes due now that I was no longer going to be part of the "tax-exempt" community. I sold it to a Wycliffe missionary who kept it in good running order until all the taxes were paid on it. Why Wycliffe had more of a tax-exempt status than HCJB Global (now Reach Beyond), I never understood. God, in His goodness, allowed me to buy it back again.

On June 8, 1973, I became a short-term missionary. The decision to be a regular missionary with HCJB Global would come in the next 18 months. I began to see God answer prayer in ways I never would have imagined. But none of the blessings would have come if I had not cut the cord with the Foreign Service and begun a life of faith. My search for a meaningful life had truly begun.

Mom and Dad in my Apartment

The surprise of my life was seeing my dad and mom get off the plane in Quito. They came to see what the mission was like and what I had given myself to for the next years of my life, wanting to make sure they were OK with my huge job change. They were so open to attending choir rehearsals, concerts, radio programs, and participating in everything that it was a huge blessing. We even took in a Mission Aviation Fellowship (MAF) flight to Limoncocha, Wycliffe's jungle base, and had a few days with our hosts. Several months before my parents made the decision to come to Quito, I asked Dad if he could provide some barrels for an older couple who had just been married and would need barrels to return to the field. Dad gladly provided what was needed, and what a treat it was for all of us! Their trip encouraged them that God is with us.

Dad's health was not good and Roger Reimer made sure he had oxygen for the nights, as the altitude in Quito is 9,300 feet. He was a serious diabetic, and legally blind, but he showed his love for me by sticking it out despite his health issues. They went home hoping that his health would improve enough so that they could do something together for the Lord.

As a missionary, I learned how to make things do, substitute for what I wanted, began sewing again, and learned how to make meals from scratch. On my next trip back from the U.S., I returned prepared to begin canning, like my mom used to. Adapting recipes to the altitude was an art, and Almeta Christiansen, hostess of the guesthouse, gave me her way of adjusting food for the high altitude. Thankfully, it worked! Barney Cook told me how to make beef brisket, and others passed on cookie recipes that did not go flat like a pancake. However, chocolate chip cookies—a standby—were never the same at this altitude.

Through Gates of Splendor, written by Elisabeth Elliot, was in my grandparents' home in Detroit. It truly captivated me and was the first book I read that I could not put down, reading into the night during high school days. I brought Dad's copy to read while visiting my grandparents in Detroit. Mom, my brothers, my sister and I were enjoying a few days with my mother's parents and relatives. It challenged me for the rest of my life. Having a friend who flew in and out of the Waorani Indian tribe, I made contact with Betty Shumate who was coordinating a tour of Ecuador with me. It was a great tour group, and several of our missionaries helped with meals, leading the hospital tour, the engineering tour at Pifo and Papallacta Dam, along with language groups preparing programs.

The Mike Ross family from Susie's home church in Ohio take Betty Shumate and me to the gravesite of the 5 young missionaries killed by the Waorani Indians in the jungle of Ecuador in 1956

One of the highlights of my years in Ecuador was traveling on an Mission Aviation Fellowship (MAF) plane over the jungle where the Waorani Indian tribe ed. Elisabeth Elliot and Rachel Saint had spent many years working on transcribing the language into written words that could be taught to the Indians with a New Testament in their language in 1992.

Five young married missionary men from different missions prayed for this tribe and decided to make an attempt to reach it by dropping gifts from Nate Saint's plane in hope that the tribal members would send something back opening a friendship. Nate Saint, husband of Marj Saint Van Der Puy and brother to Rachel

Saint, was the jungle pilot who discovered where this tribe was located. It was considered a hidden tribe in the Ecuadorian jungle. After making many contacts back and forth, not knowing how the Waorani thought, rather than gain their trust, the airplane caused a fear in the tribe, ultimately leading to the deaths of the five men. This horrifying incident caused many other missionaries I have met to seriously consider going to the mission field, just the opposite of what would be expected. What a privilege it was to fly into the jungle with Mike, a missionary pilot from my home church in Cleveland, Ohio. When they arrived in Quito, I had invited them to spend a night or two to get everything organized to fly to Shell where they would be living with their baby.

On a recent trip to Cleveland with my husband, Dwight, we went to church at Parkside Chapel, where we saw Mike and Joan standing at a missions table in the lobby. They are still active in missions. After hearing nothing about them in probably 25 years or more, it was encouraging to see God had kept them in missions.

Harry Yeoman, my first boss at Reach Beyond

In 1990 my friend Olive Fleming Liefeld, widow of Peter Fleming who was one of the five missionaries martyred in Ecuador, wrote *Unfolding Destinies—The Untold Story of Peter Fleming and the Auca Mission*. It was a book with answers Olive had waited for most of her life. Olive states, "Dawa and Kimo returned to their story, picking up from when the men were killed." 'They heard singing,' Rachel said, puzzled. Walt and I looked at each other. 'Who was singing? The five men?' Rachel asked them my question. Dawa's answer was, 'No, their dead bodies were lying on the beach.' So who was singing? But Rachel was concentrating too deeply to answer. 'After the men were killed, Dawa in the woods and Kimo on the beach heard singing,' Rachel said. 'As they looked up over the treetops they saw a large group of people. They were all singing, and it looked as if there were a hundred flashlights.'

"Rachel explained, 'This is the only word for "bright light" that they know. But they said it was very bright and flashing. Then suddenly it disappeared.'

'Were they talking about angels? Was it possible that he (sic) had used the men's fatal mistake as his opportunity to break through to these natives who had been bound by such incredible darkness and evil?' Dawa later indicated it was so. She told Rachel that the vision was what first led her to believe that there was a God. And when Betty and Rachel and Dayuma (who had become a Christian) eventually arrived, Dawa had become the first Christian in the tribe."

After I had been with the mission a couple of years, it was possible for me to repurchase my Volkswagen from the Wycliffe missionary who had bought it. He was returning to the U.S. and gave me a good price that I could afford. How wonderful it is to have a car in a foreign city!

Radio station HCJB focused on broadcasting in 1931, but over the years locals came to the mission for medical help, and a clinic was started, then a hospital in Quito was born several years later. Medical missionaries joined with Ecuadorian professionals to fill all the needs of a hospital while equipment was given from donors in various countries. A second hospital was born in Shell. Often MAF missionaries would fly people from the jungle to Shell to receive medical care.

Everyone I met in Quito had been extremely well trained in their field and could have made a lot of money working in the U.S. They all had a desire to serve the Lord where He called them. Each one was unique and delightful to work with and learn from.

During my eight years in Quito, I worked with the U.S. Embassy the first year, and the last seven years I served as a short-term missionary, supporting myself the first six months, then encouraging friends from everywhere to send gifts to the mission for my support, as my personal savings were being depleted. It was most encouraging! Harry and May Yeoman were the main reason I asked if there a job for me to do with HCJB. One of the first support gifts came from a friend I met in a Virginia church while working in Washington, D.C. She and her husband were the first to send support to the mission for my monthly expenses. My home church was very slow to officially support me, but many of the congregation helped me individually—it is funny how we mistake what God is doing. God touches hearts of people we least expect. Gradually, I learned more and more about living a life of faith. Prayer was a daily must, sometimes hourly. Oh, there is so much to learn about trusting God.

It was my opportunity to work as secretary for the broadcast side of the mission for Harry Yeoman, Ben Cummings, Tom Fulghum, Roger Stubbe, Sam Rowley, Herb Jacobson and John Christiansen; then on the healthcare side I worked for Carl Wilhelm (a great boss), Sara Risser, Craig Shuck, Ruth Ann De Flon, Dr. Gil Wagoner and Dr. Ev Bruckner. What a learning curve! Opportunities, everywhere.

Outside of my regular work as a personal secretary, wonderful opportunities came my way via a tour of the mission and Ecuador, for a meal or overnight. Many of us were asked to sing in a choir for Quito Day events in schools, parks and even in the Presidential Palace downtown. We were tired and cold, but happy with the audience's response everywhere we went. During those days Gene Jordan directed the choir. Tom Fulghum selected the smaller groups to sing in Sunday-night ensembles for the evening *Back Home Hour* radio program that aired via shortwave. Opportunities, everywhere.

One year I was asked to organize a Christmas lunch for all of our Ecuadorian employees. A seasoned missionary lady helped me make the plans, meat was ordered, and missionaries signed up for everything that would make the lunch complete. Dwight's late wife, Lynne, made the best contribution from a missionary wife—a huge tub of coleslaw! What a lady! I will never forget the hard work it took, but we sure had great missionaries! A senior missionary gave me some advice: "You have to provide bread or they will feel we have not given them a complete meal." We must have fed more than 75 that day.

Imagine trying to raise a tower via the cantilever method on the side of Mt. Pichincha that reaches over 15,000 feet in height and overshadows the entire city of Quito. Pichincha is a giant, the length of the city of Quito. It is cold all the time and can be rainy high on Pichincha, which makes the terrain slippery, and the job of raising a tower for the radio station requires a dump truck with a nervous driver and a winch to pull everything in his direction. Oh, and the front of his truck is a little off the ground! Pretty scary! Herb Jacobson was in charge of the tower raising. He spoke more rapidly than I had ever heard him do before when he thought the tower might go beyond straight up.

In 1979 it was time for my second home ministry assignment to thank churches and donors and give them updates of how people have had their lives changed. While I was staying with Tassie Law, a lovely Scottish widow in Evanston, Illinois, an early-morning call came from Dr. Van Der Puy, then president of HCJB (Reach Beyond). He asked if I would cut my furlough very quickly and come to Miami to work for him because his secretary was too ill to continue. I asked for a day to think about it (because I enjoyed the healthcare side of the ministry). After prayer and discussion with Tassie, I agreed to cut my travel short and drive to Miami.

Dr. Van Der Puy was the most delightful man I ever worked with—extremely kind and wise. During that time I was moved from one mobile home to another on the mission property. I do not believe I have ever seen so many snakes anywhere I have ever lived as in Miami. Wanting to have some stability in my life, I looked and prayed about renting an apartment.

One of my colleagues invited me to dinner to see her mobile home. She was planning on retiring to California and offered me a good price for her furnished home. I bought it. It was my home until the mission moved to Colorado Springs in 1992.

After two years of visiting various churches, a lady in the home office invited me to go to Key Biscayne Presbyterian Church. After a few visits, I became a member and drove myself back and forth from Opa Locka (a city near Miami on the edge of a drug-infested area) to lovely Key Biscayne. Eventually, I developed an interest in the missions program at the church and agreed to serve as a secretary. I enjoyed making friends with people outside of the mission. In Quito we had a huge group of expatriate friends to do things with, but in Miami at the end of the work day, we drove home until the next work day. It took me time to make new friends.

Dr. Van Der Puy stepped down as President, shifting his energy to other mission-related projects. We had worked together very well, so he asked the board if I could be available to help him sending letters to raise funds for the new project of placing Spanish-language radio stations along the U.S.-México border from Brownsville, Texas, to Yuma, Arizona. Eventually it became the World Radio Network (now called Inspiracom). Miami had been my home for 12 years. During that time I was always available to work for Dr. Van Der Puy, at the board's request. I finished my bachelor's degree in English at Florida International University on August 10, 1990, just after I celebrated my 50th birthday in Miami.

After Dr. Van Der Puy no longer needed a full-time secretary, I was asked to work in Quito and Miami for John Christiansen (the mission's board secretary) when necessary. Over the years in Miami I served for several men: Mac McCloud, John Osborne, Dale Shuck, then Dick Jacquin. The Miami location became dangerous when more crime started touching the edge of the mission property, and the board unanimously agreed to relocate the mission elsewhere. The choice was to relocate to Colorado Springs.

We moved to Colorado Springs, where I bought my first home, and enjoyed living there for 17 years. Every year I did one little thing to improve the value of my house. During those years in Colorado Springs I branched out into communications work, preparing items for the printers, translating documents from Spanish to English, taking calls in Spanish for the receptionists, ghost-writing letters to send to donors with updates on key projects, helping with vision journeys and updating historical files.

Village Seven Presbyterian Church was my home church in Colorado Springs. After being a member a few years, I was selected with others for training to help identify needs, whether congregational counseling by one or two of us, or if the problem needed to be referred to a professional counselor. We met weekly for several months, doing role-playing to put ourselves on both sides. One of the ladies in our group was in charge of teaching soldiers to fly using a simulator with all possible events encountered in case of combat. What an amazing woman she is! She supported me when I went to South Africa. Her husband had died while I was in South Africa, but we had a wonderful visit when I took Dwight to meet her after I returned to Colorado Springs, just before we were married.

Serving in hospitality is something I've enjoyed most wherever I lived. I enjoy looking at photos of those who have stayed with me for up to six months at a time. It has always been part of what I enjoy doing to get to know people. Many times I felt blessed to have had guests in my home.

Our church had large groups of women's Bible studies taught by well-prepared ladies. Being a part of this group was essential to my life in Colorado Springs. After a few seasons, I was asked if I would take the next year. Isaiah has become someone I feel so sorry for after working on that book of the Bible for 1½ years. But we all learned so much! The next year I taught was a delight—the story of Ruth, Naomi and Boaz. God shows us so many things in Scripture that we need to hide in our heart until we can share them with others.

Avril and John Thomas made all of my time in South Africa fruitful and a Blessing

As the years went by, I felt more out of place as a missionary working in an office in the U.S. Feeling that I would "die" if I did not serve overseas again, in 2003 I joined a work team from Indiana for two weeks to Cape Town, South Africa. The mission had been partnering with Living Hope for several years, and I wanted to see the work. It was a busy time, full of unexpected ways of serving the Lord. The last day in Cape Town, I told Avril Thomas I knew the Lord wanted me back doing whatever was needed. I had no idea what. We agreed to pray about an open door.

Avril's husband, Pastor John Thomas, contacted me by email asking me to be his wife's personal assistant. By June 2004 the Lord provided funds to cover my support deficit with the mission and enough extra to cover expenses for two years living in Cape Town. Funds also came in for my travel expenses. I arrived in Cape Town to work with Avril Thomas who was director of CCFM, a Christian radio station that our mission had helped start after apartheid was over and Nelson Mandela became president of South Africa.

The first year I helped Avril wind up her directorship of CCFM. Peter and Nancy Brown had a cozy two-bedroom home in Fish Hoek, and were willing to rent it to me for two years. They also loaned me their car until I could find one to buy. Such provision!

My job was personal secretary to Avril Thomas at CCFM, putting papers in order for a possible new radio station manager in the near future. I made graphs of our monthly income, expenses, the number of listeners, so that in six months we had an idea how well the funds were coming in to sustain the radio station. What a great group of employees to work with.

CCFM listenership had grown and it was time for Avril to concentrate on the Living Hope homeless ministry across the street that she started. Once a week I took notes during meetings at the homeless center, but the rest of the week I took notes for several meetings at CCFM. It took three months to understand the way the "colored" people spoke with their trills and accent. The Afrikaaners had a different accent than that, but the British I understood thanks to BBC TV!

The tribal groups had names that were hard to spell, let alone speak. So I really worked on pronouncing names correctly. The British-background folk were the easiest to understand, but Afrikaans is derived from the form of Dutch brought to the Cape by Protestant settlers in the 17th century, and became one of the official languages of South Africa.

Soon, I began helping across the street at the Homeless Centre each morning. Someone started a song, and I found it on the keyboard and played as many verses as they knew. We had a lot of laughs and many hearts that were open to the gospel. Soup was the menu each day as local stores provided. I often drove to the butcher in Fish Hoek to see what was available for the group. It was humbling, but wonderful to see how willing people were to donate.

There were groups not just in townships that needed to be contacted, such as a senior care center with some very grateful ladies who appreciated a time of prayer, discussing health issues, etc. Gradually, I put together several binders with photos and medical information from the Internet for each group leader after our medical staff gave it the "OK" for use. The main issues were AIDS, lung issues, cleanliness, healthy eating, and the necessity of having peanut butter on hand when meat is not available to one's small budget, and when to go to the clinic.

As time went by, and I made friends with these leaders. I talked more about their faith and what grounded it. This especially applied to new believers who needed to begin good habits of reading the Bible, praying, and depending on God to answer. Some like Maggie changed their lives, but others drifted away. Avril knew more about them than I did, but we were encouraged when a few little changes here and there were visible in their lives. It was great to have a small part.

Avril surprised me with an invitation to join her for a ladies' luncheon at church; rarely did I leave the office unless it was for a medical appointment or vacation. Avril emphasized that it was part of my job to mingle among the ladies of the church and take speaking engagements when I was asked. What freedom! From then on, when the wind blew through my hair I felt free like never before. This was the beginning of the most wonderful, fruitful experience I had as a missionary, and the Lord blessed me through many hard moments.

My visa was up in July 2006, and I had no choice at that time but to return to the U.S. on March 6, 2006, and apply for another visa. An anonymous person organized a dinner for about 30 friends on a ship in the Navy Yard that served meals for special occasions.

Friends of John and Avril Thomas in Africa treated all these friends for my first farewell the Navy Yard in Simons Town, S. Africa.

Returning to the mission headquarters in Colorado Springs in July, a new employee who did not know me at all, informed me that I was only entitled to three months of home leave, and I needed to choose to *"retire or find a job at the mission."* What a "gobsmack" that was! I was flabbergasted that none of my work schedule was in any file. I had sent back to headquarters all my work days, days of vacation, and sick days—what the mission requested, but this employee never even asked me how many days of vacation I had taken, or if I had taken home leave in the last two years. The personnel director was not available that week, so I never had a chance to talk with her. I asked Ed Giesbrecht, a former boss, what I should do. He was kind to give me back my old job as his secretary until I received my new visa to return to South Africa.

Not knowing how long I would need to wait for a new visa, I stayed with friends for a month while I arranged for my furniture to be returned to my house, cleaning it up from top to bottom. I replaced the carpet, painted the walls, and spent money I did not want to at this time in my life. What a stressful time! After setting up house, I enjoyed five months working for Ed Giesbrecht. A new visa was granted seven months later in October 2006. It was time to go back to Cape Town.

As soon as I found someone in church who would be glad to store my belongings for two years, I booked a flight with a work team back to Cape Town on March 7, 2007, and eased into the work with Avril again by being part of the work team. During the work team two weeks, I heard of an apartment. It was just what I needed when the work team returned, so I saw it and rented it. Avril had arranged for me to work more with the people in several townships. That made my last two years the *best* and the *hardest*. God was so good! Two men at the homeless center and later two ladies in a group meeting at a township church wanted to accept Jesus, and I was just there when God touched their hearts so I could pray with them. What a rich time that was, especially to see two of them changed over time through God's grace. My direct contact with people in the townships was fulfilling and depressing.

One day I had the urge to go to Capricorn Township to call on a couple whose daughter had been kidnapped and killed in another part of Africa. The wife was home alone with a baby that was suffering from asthma. She was so afraid that God would take this child from her that she held the baby while she made tea for us. I prayed. I also promised I would check with her each time I was in Capricorn. Her husband had contacts who referred them to a children's hospital in Cape Town. Avril had us take any in our groups who wanted training for children's medical care. It was quite a hairy drive, but we got there! Each person in my car learned something that applied to their township and felt happy about the teaching received.

Maggie asked me to help her open a bank account, which I did. She smiled when she had her bank information in her hand. She went through her good and bad days many times before I left, but I invited her to have a lunch during my last week in Fish Hoek. She enjoyed the meal. Then I said to her, "Maggie, you are the only one who can reach the children in your township. You know when a parent has died from AIDS, when they need food, have no one to pay for school. You know who to tell these problems to at Living Hope to fix it. There is just one thing that would make you even more effective in your neighborhood. You show your anger too quickly to others, then they get afraid of you.

She asked me if I would take her home and stop at a store on the way first so she could make her last payment on a washing machine. I said, "Sure!" So we looked at the ATM and she looked at me and said, "Can I get my money out of that machine?" "Absolutely!" I said. So I coached her through the process, and when the money came out in her hand, she looked amazed. Such a delight!

Avril and John Thomas are the couple who made this all happen. I thank them for their long-suffering as I adapted to what was needed. On July 2, 2008, I left Cape Town at age 68 and returned to Colorado Springs to retire from HCJB Global which became Reach Beyond. Though I had prayed for God's direction in my retirement years, I had no guidance, no inkling what I might do. I had written to my church in Colorado Springs offering to visit the ill and homebound—those who were dying, or wherever they needed help in visitation. I heard nothing back. The church was going through some changes. A Scripture René read on my farewell the last Sunday in South Africa was Psalm 2:13-14: *I am still confident of this: I will see the goodness of the Lord in the land of the living. Wait for the Lord; be strong and take heart and wait for the Lord."* That kept me going from day to day. My goal was to retire after 26 years of service with Reach Beyond, and I made it, with many wonderful memories, with several different tasks over the years. But the last was the best.

CHAPTER 22

A New Life Begins

Once I was back home, after collecting my furniture for a second time, painting walls, and redoing the woodwork again, I began to feel at home. After 26 years with HCJB Global (now Reach Beyond), I was officially retired. And I was home just in time for the Fourth of July—my goal.

When my computer was connected and my email was back online, a string of messages came in. Instantly, I was connected to friends and felt encouraged. One of the messages was from Dwight Lind whose wife passed away while I was in Cape Town. He understood what it was like to come back home and changes in your church, local friends leaving, friends gone to heaven, gives a feeling of disconnectedness. What he said was like water from a far country. It spoke to my heart.

A month later Dwight came to Colorado Springs for a dinner to thank donors for gifts to a project in an Arizona town called Sierra Vista. Tom Fulghum gave me a personal invitation to attend the dinner at the mission's headquarters. Because I didn't know about the project and had not given to it, I felt out of place. But I agreed to help in the kitchen, making coffee and cleaning up. Uncomfortable about Dwight's being present after his writing such a lovely email, I dragged my feet and rewashed a coffee pot, hoping Dwight might have left. But he had not. He was waiting in the parking lot with some others. After some conversation, he invited me to have lunch or supper with him the next day. Before I could say, "I don't know." I heard myself say, "Sure, that would be nice."

We had a relaxing time enjoying a sandwich at the Garden of the Gods, comparing interests and sharing our mission connection, to the point that I invited him to come to my home for coffee or tea. He asked if I would mind if he called once in a while just to have someone to talk with. After several months of chatting on Skype, Dwight sent a message that he would be with his grown children during the holidays, but would send me a message after New Year's Day when he returned to Sierra Vista. I could leave him a message to read when he got home in Arizona.

His proposal was sent with a box of lovely roses and chocolate. The note said, "This is my you-know-what, will you?" I was so sure God had put us together that there was no question in my mind, and I said, "Yes!" By the time the mission got around to having a retirement farewell for me, Dwight was in town staying at Andy and Linda Braio's place and able to attend. What a celebration it was for me to have him there!

We were married June 20, 2009, in the little chapel at Flying W Ranch in Colorado Springs. The small chapel was full. It was a wonderful beginning to a blessed life together. Both of my brothers came by train from Ohio, a few life-long friends came, and many mission colleagues. By mission standards, I had to come out of my short retirement, for us to continue as a couple Reach Beyond. I sent a short list of what I would be glad to do: hosting staff for overnights as needed—equipment repairs were fairly often—traveling with Dwight when he had to visit stations under his care in El Paso, TX; Douglas, Nogales, and Yuma, in Arizona. It dusted my Spanish. We still visit the staff when they celebrate a big anniversary. Dwight retired in 2012, so that gave me 3 more years for a total of 29 with Reach Beyond.

Every day we thank God for bringing us together. Our lives have been full doing things together from working on loan to Inspiracom, to visiting family, friends and supporting churches. We even visited Cape Town in 2013 where Dwight met John and Avril Thomas, Maggie, Bongiwe, and many others who made my time in South Africa so very special. Only God knows the rest of the story, but we know how it ends—walking through the pearly gates of heaven.

Four years after our wedding, Dwight and I flew to South Africa to meet the people I had worked with. John and Avril Thomas invited Maggie, along with many others I wanted Dwight to meet. René drove Maggie home with us, so we could see her washing machine, Dwight pointed to two places on the wall where there were photos of me with Maggie. Wow! Avril assured me she was still working with people who needed help. She has come a long way.

A young lady named Bongiwe accepted the Lord one day at a small group meeting. She struggled with her life in the township she lived in. When her baby was a year old, and she wanted to celebrate her life, she invited me for some tea and dessert. She had running cold water, but had to use an outhouse. Her room was so cold I wondered how she managed. I gave her money for clothing and food for her baby until she got established as a nurse's aide at the Living Hope Clinic which is within walking distance.

René, our hostess, invited Bongiwe to join us for a meal so Dwight could meet her. She has had many ups and downs, but she is strong in her faith in Jesus now. She planned to go back to her homeland where her mother is caring for her other children. I pray she has had her needs met and is still depending on the Lord for her children's futures.

To be sure Dwight saw Cape Point, Irmgard, who had been in charge of radio programming (in the town of Muizenberg), took us for a "tea" break. What an absolute delight! We climbed the steps up to the lighthouse for photos, then enjoyed our tea break near the sea at Cape Point. Irmgard lost her husband after I left, so it was special to have time with her. She has retired from CCFM. She was fun to be with, and Dwight was overwhelmed by her kindness and yummy snacks. Then she took us to see wild life within the Cape Point and the most beautiful zebras anywhere.

Peter and Nancy Brown, a couple Dwight and I both knew through Reach Beyond in Colorado Springs, invited us to have a meal with them in the cottage I rented from them the first two years I lived in South Africa near Fish Hoek. We have been friends for a long time.

Living Way is the organization built by John and Avril Thomas who pastored King of Kings Baptist Centre until until he began he began managing Living Way together with Avril. The desire of Living Way is to teach people a way to make a living on their own. When we were there a huge emphasis was on horticulture, something that has been very successful—so successful that vegetables grown have been sold in the mall's grocery store. Another ministry was sewing—anything from clothing to bags made of beautiful fabric. Also, sculpting with wood and pottery, as well as many other artistic projects depending on the people willing to participate with their skills.

Before we returned to the U.S., Peter and Barbara invited us to spend a day with them, have a picnic in Franschhoek, where groups of Huguenots from France settled in stages. In 1948 a museum and a beautiful garden with pillars around a pond make a lovely tribute to the Dutch people who have made South Africa their home. Many of the Dutch built their own houses, as you can see in the museum. Franschhoek is a lovely part of South Africa.

While we were in Fish Hoek we contacted Pam, a native of Zimbabwe Dwight met while in Malawi. Dwight, along with another Reach Beyond missionary and two others, flew there to build a TV studio for African Bible College. Pam was attending a course at YWAM's (Youth With a Mission) communications program in South Africa at the time. We treated her to a meal at a restaurant with a view. She is back in Malawi now, and we are glad to have a part in supporting her.

It was a little easier to say goodbye to South Africa this time, because I had Dwight in my life. God has blessed us and we have been able to visit most of our friends whom God has given us throughout the years more than once. Our trip to South Africa was a huge blessing for both of us. Thank you, Lord, for your provision, love, guidance and amazing patience with me over these 84 years. Yes, these are the best years.

René was our hostess for a month! Dwight and I tried to do quiet things in her garden while she slept during the day. It worked out pretty well, and Rene got her needed sleep. Rene's brother and daughter and their spouses all gave us wonderful meals like the photos recorded for us. Thank you, René!

No matter where you go, if you have accepted Jesus Christ as your Savior, you will have
His guidance and provision—whatever that may be—to show you the way planned for
you. He removes the water bugs and replaces all with His love for each of us.

Susie Lind

Printed in the United States
by Baker & Taylor Publisher Services